How to Be on a Diet for 45 Years and Never Be Thin

A Practical Guide to Freedom and Happiness

Tami Muller

How to Be on a Diet for 45 Years and Never Be Thin
A Practical Guide to Freedom and Happiness

Tami Muller

English Adaptation: Gabriel Muller
Design: Einav Shachar
Publishing: Tami Muller
Miami 2024
www.tamimuller.com

ISBN 9798218333348

Table of Contents

To Dani, who loves me unconditionally and at any weight.

To Gabriel, Yoni, and Avia, who, thankfully, did not inherit my flaws.

To mom and dad - I owe my story to you (for good and bad).

Preface

Nice to Meet You. I'm Tami Muller, and I'm on a Diet

He was the most handsome officer in my Israeli Defense Force unit. Every day, I would go to collect the unit's top-secret mail in a brown bag, and there he was, standing tall and tanned, nonchalantly playing with his silver chain and watching the parade of girls float by. As they strolled past, they threw him flirtatious glances. Maybe I did too, but I can't quite remember. All I know is that I felt invisible.

One day, out of the blue, I heard him say, "So, what did you say your name was?" I quickly looked around, but there was no one behind me, in front of me, or at my side. Was he talking to me?

I gathered my wits and said, "I didn't say, but my name's Tami," blushing to the roots of my fiery red hair.

"Nice name," he said, giving me an amused look. "My niece is also named Tami." He toyed with his necklace and continued, "Want to have dinner tonight?"

And so, as simple as that, this total catch asked

me out on a date. I was at a loss for words. I had spent months devising witty retorts and playful comebacks for this exact scenario, but now that it was happening, I was speechless. I looked him in the eyes and, without hesitation, said, "I can't. I'm on a diet."

"What diet?" he inquired, as if he had some deep familiarity with the subject.

"Scarsdale," I blurted out, immediately regretting the overshare.

"Well, what's on the menu for today?" as though aware the diet had daily variations.

"Fish and green beans," I skeptically replied.

"Great, why don't you come over to my place and I'll cook it for you."

That's how it all began. I went to his place, he cooked us dinner, and we ended up dating for seven years. I lost 15 pounds (and then we broke up and I gained back those 15, plus another 10).

Nice to meet you; I'm Tami Muller, and I'm on a diet.

Chapter 1

What Do I Know from Happiness Studies?

"I'm on a Diet."

This is the sentence I have repeated more than any other in my life, in all languages and styles. Indeed, I have been on one diet or another for over 45 years. Am I thin? Absolutely not. Not yet, at least. Just yesterday, I indulged in a hearty cheeseburger, accompanied by sweet potato fries and a cold bottle of grapefruit juice, the kind that reminds me of my childhood days in a sleepy suburb of Tel Aviv. But who's counting, anyway?

While savoring my beloved cheeseburger, I stumbled upon an article about a new weight loss injection and, without hesitation, immediately called my doctor for a prescription.

"It's just that I have a wedding soon," I pleaded, wiping the ketchup off my chin. "It's more or less medically necessary."

No, I didn't attend my high school reunion; I couldn't fit in my jeans. Yes, I know, I'm approaching 60, and

I look good and feel great. So, what exactly is the big deal? I've been married for 33 years—happily most of the time (to a different catch, not the one from the army)—and I'm a mother to three wonderful adults. After 30 years of climbing the corporate ladder, I decided with my husband to cash in our chips and travel the world together, making every moment count. I teach happiness, give talks to auditoriums full of students, and try to do good for others. I cherish life as it unfolds. Truly.

So, what's my issue? Why is this so important to me? Why am I driving myself crazy? Oh, and I'm also perfectly healthy, so there's really no reason to go crazy.

And yet, here I am, going crazy.

I've Always Wanted to Be Thin

Even as a little girl, I would look at my thin, flat-tummied friends with envy. They had the perfect dimples on their lower backs that I would have done anything for. While they proudly showed off their bikinis on the beach, I was confined to a full-body swimsuit, topped off with a T-shirt for good measure (only lying down or standing, never sitting!). They were slim, blonde, and athletic, while I was chubby, freckled, and redheaded.

They played basketball, and I played the piano. They laughed with boys, and I chatted with the librarian. But even then, it was clear to me that I would stop at nothing to achieve that flat stomach and fit into size two shorts.

Over the years, I tried everything: diets, pills, injections, liposuction, and even a mini tummy tuck. But no matter what I did, I never felt satisfied. I tried every diet imaginable Scarsdale, Atkins, no bread, only bread, cabbage soup, high protein, ketogenic, the 4-Hour, the 17-Day, paleo, Muscle Builder, hypnosis, and sugar withdrawal. Enough already, I'm getting tired (of writing, not dieting).

Perpetually Almost Ready

I'm constantly almost ready: for a high school reunion or a relative's wedding, I'm always on the verge of being ready for the next big event. Each year on my birthday, I tell myself that this will be the year I finally look young and fit. But here I am, 20 pounds away from my October birthday, with time slipping through my fingers. Rosh Hashanah, the Jewish New Year, has already passed, and the indulgent meals of brisket and apples with honey have derailed my grand plans. Now I'm frantically searching the internet, desperately seeking answers on how to lose 20 pounds in just two weeks.

Turning 30, 40, and 50 should be milestones worth celebrating, especially for someone like me, who loves festivities and joy. But those years passed much like they came. And now, here I am, touching 60, still carrying the same weight. I gaze at the little black dress I bought for those long-awaited milestones, the tags still clinging to it, and I sheepishly return it to the closet, thinking, "Maybe next year."

But something has shifted in recent years. Suddenly, I have had an epiphany: I am happy. Not always, but mostly. I am finding joy in my life, regardless of my weight or my desire to lose it. I am starting to understand that my identity is not solely determined by my body, especially not by its size. Throughout six decades, my body and mind have faithfully served me, providing good health, resilience, energy, and an incredible memory (my husband even claims that I remember things that never happened!). I have a sensitive and musical ear, a curious mind, broad shoulders, a generous hand, a strong back, good posture, and a proud, sensitive nose that delights in pleasant scents. I have a refined palate that appreciates complex flavors, compassionate eyes that truly see people for who they are, and, most importantly, a big heart brimming with love, wonder, and gratitude for all that life has given me.

Don't get me wrong: my desire to lose 20 pounds hasn't disappeared, but I've realized that it no longer determines my happiness or controls my life. In the positive psychology field, this is known as "active acceptance." We accept ourselves as we are while also striving to improve. Life isn't simply black and white; it's multi-dimensional, and that's what makes it beautiful. We can desire something without being dependent on it. We can embrace this paradox because it adds depth to our lives. I accept myself, including my wrinkles and cellulite. While I may not love every aspect of my body, I love myself regardless. I focus on the things that truly matter to me: being more attentive, giving more, playing more, laughing more, learning more, teaching more, and savoring every moment. Miraculously, I find myself happier.

There's a reason this book isn't titled *How to Be On A Diet for 45 Years and Not Lose Weight.* I have indeed lost weight, multiple times. I've been 20 pounds lighter and felt on top of the world when I fit into my eighth-grade jeans and confidently strutted in five-inch stilettos. But this happiness was short-lived because I still didn't like myself any better. The photos looked fantastic, but I still felt incomplete. The truth is the barrier between me and happiness wasn't 20 pounds; it was me. It was all of me when I put my life on hold and didn't know how to live in the present moment. I was standing in my own way.

So, I made the decision to live authentically, without pretending or forcing myself to conform to a specific image. This is who I am, with all my strengths, weaknesses, beauty, and areas for growth. I have no patience for insincerity or hidden agendas. I don't pass judgment on others and don't want to be judged either. Our time on Earth is limited, so there's no point in waiting until I lose weight, earn more money, achieve success, see my child get married, or watch my bank account grow.

Life is happening right now, and I want to live it fully without hiding. So, I'll attend my next high school reunion wearing a flattering blouse, go to the beach because it brings me joy, and take a Pilates class even if I spend most of it sitting on the mat, envious of the 25-year-olds next to me who can fold in half from their navels. I won't waste any more time!

In this book, you won't find the magic solution to being thin—I haven't discovered it myself yet. You will, however, find humor, compassion, and vulnerability alongside actions and small changes that have worked for me and made my life happier. These interventions have made me more resilient, enabling me to overcome hardships and obstacles along the way. Yes, I've had my fair share of those, too.

This book is really a twist on all the "How to Lose Weight" books out there. I don't have the answers, but I also don't want to wait until I do, because there are more important things I want to share with you.

Writing this book has healed me in many ways and provided me with perspective and appreciation for my life. Although the desire to be thin still exists, I now approach it differently. I no longer let it control my life. These days, I strive to be in control by using the tools and insights I have gained from my studies in the science of happiness and positive psychology.

These tools include self-love, self-compassion, reframing, leveraging my strengths, and practicing gratitude. You can find more about these techniques in this book.

So I invite you to join me, let your belly out (metaphorically, or not . . .), and laugh a little (not too much; they say laughing is fattening). Let's embark together on a fun trip (journey always sounded tiring to me . . .) towards freedom and happiness, even if we haven't reached our desired goal yet.

☛ How I Found Myself Working in a Job I Didn't Like

Bob Dylan sings, "What's a sweetheart like you doing in a dump like this?" And many people ask me the same thing: What is someone like you, with degrees in economics and business administration, realistic and practical, doing in the happiness and spirituality field? (Usually asked with a hint of skepticism). How did you end up here?

For more than 30 years, I lived in the business world, working in finance, business development, marketing, and sales management. I was successful, but I didn't find fulfillment in my work. I felt like something was missing. I immigrated to Florida with my parents, to Toronto with my sister and her family, and back to Miami after my beloved father passed away suddenly from cardiac arrest at age 59. I couldn't come to terms with the loss and the void it left, and I sought answers and reasons. I swapped my business management books for spiritual ones; I tried meditation but without much success. I did, however, find comfort in the new world revealed to me, even if I wasn't sure what to do with it yet.

One day, I attended the funeral of a member of my community. In the eulogies, his friends and family all spoke of how much he had helped and contributed to those around him, changing their lives in profound ways. I couldn't help but wonder, what will they say about me when I'm gone? That I was a marketing and business development mogul? Whom did I help? Whom did I make a difference for? It was then that I knew it was time for a change. I wanted something more meaningful.

Throughout my life, I've been repeatedly encouraged to pursue a career that involves helping others. I tried to understand what everyone was telling me. Perhaps I should study alternative medicine? I enrolled in a local university at the age of 45, only to realize that despite my interest, I wouldn't be able to legally practice in Florida with that degree, and I dropped out (retaining my extensive knowledge of herbology). Maybe Chinese medicine? But the program being offered was seven years long, and the nearest college was a four-hour drive away. Reflexology? I don't really vibe with feet.

And so, I continued my search, exploring and reading, trying to understand how I could make a difference. How could I help people? I was determined to find my calling, my purpose, and make a true impact in the world.

Then, on one of my trips back to Israel, I reconnected with my dear friend Dr. Moshe Ben-Eliezer (Mushi), who had known me since I was 19, when I was his direct report in the IDF.

I was undisciplined, argumentative, and defiant, but according to him, I did a great job when needed, despite my flaws. He really does know me well and I valued his wisdom and advice.

"Ginger," he said. "Maybe you should be a happiness coach?"

I looked at him, astonished, jaw dropped. "Happiness coach? Are you completely out of your mind?"

"Absolutely not," he replied. "It's a fascinating field. One can study happiness in universities these days and you were really born for it."

But how could I possibly tell everyone back home that I was going to be a happiness coach? After all, the degrees in economics and business administration sounded so much more impressive (to my mother for sure). I listened to his advice, internalized it, and enjoyed the rest of my visit to Israel. But something inside me wouldn't let it go. I knew that there was an entire world out there that I didn't know about, and it was pulling me in like a magnet. But I had done nothing to make it my reality yet.

I returned to the United States and to my marketing career. I continued to meet with clients, drink cocktails, wear suits and high heels, feel financially secure, and ignore that little voice inside me that urged me to explore.

Coincidence? Or, How I Met Dr. Tal Ben-Shahar

Little by little, I discovered the world of positive psychology (so what if I'd been kicked out of all my high school psychology classes and failed the Intro to Psychology course at university)?, and suddenly, the cocktails I drank with clients tasted less sweet, my feet ached more in heels, my smiles felt forced, and my successes seemed empty. It was then, 20 years after my father's death, the event that had truly changed my life, that I made the decision to take the next step. This time, it was for real. One day, while scouring Google for happiness training, happiness science, happiness courses, and so forth, I stumbled upon The Happiness Studies Academy, which offered certification for happiness trainers. I clicked on the link and was immediately captivated.

There, on the webpage, I found a name I didn't recognize—Dr. Tal Ben-Shahar. Judging by his name, I assumed he must be Israeli like me. I started filling out the registration form but had to stop because I was running late to the grand opening of a building that a close friend had constructed in Miami. Excitedly, I called my husband and told him about my discovery.

"Tal?" he asked.

"How do you know him? What do you know about

happiness studies? And what else are you keeping from me?" I responded, curious and suspicious at the same time.

"It turns out he helped incorporate happiness design elements into the building. I think he'll be at the opening tonight."

I could barely contain my excitement. Was this all just a coincidence? Out of all the websites, instructors, and events, was everything aligning at this one moment? We arrived at the opening and were greeted by a throng of people, all enjoying the beautiful surroundings, the breathtaking view, and, of course, the champagne. As soon as I stepped out of the elevator, I saw him Dr. Ben-Shahar, the man I had watched in a video just an hour before. He was surrounded by people, which made me realize that he must be an important figure among the familiar faces of Miami.

Filled with a newfound confidence, I approached him, introduced myself, and shared my story. He listened attentively, genuinely interested in what I had to say. His modest smile and kind demeanor were evident from the start. Little did I know at the time, this chance encounter would mark the beginning of a new chapter in my life. As I later discovered, he was a renowned expert in the field, but he treated me with the same respect and attention as anyone else. He suggested we talk more about my interest in the course and my new professional path, and I eagerly took him up on his offer. Our conversation led to my registration, and thus began my journey of learning and self-discovery. The course brought about a profound transformation in both my personal and professional life, finally leading me to find my true calling.

☛ The Building Blocks of Happiness That Make Me Happy

From the first day of class, everything suddenly made sense to me. I realized that all the things I had always done intuitively—practicing gratitude, appreciating beauty, acknowledging my imperfections and finding ways to compensate with my strengths, striving for happiness, giving to others and myself, constantly learning, laughing, living with perspective, and cherishing moments with loved ones—were actually all building blocks of the science of happiness. And it wasn't just intuition; these things had been scientifically researched and proven to work.

With this realization, I made the decision to take the next step and complete my training. I switched careers and became a speaker and happiness coach, dedicating myself to speaking, teaching courses, and working with clients in one-on-one settings. After completing my certification, I founded the Happiness Studies Academy Alumni & Business Club with the mission statement: The Happiness Revolution in Action. The club started with 30 pioneers and now has over 1,000 like-minded and like-hearted members in more than 70 countries, all committed to making the science of happiness accessible and bringing a little more happiness to their own homes and communities. Day by day, step by step, my goal in this book is to bring the science of happiness to you and empower you to bring a little more happiness into your own life, using the same tools that have been verified by researchers and have worked for me.

☛ Not 20 Pounds, Nor Close to It!

I've always believed that the one thing standing between me and pure happiness is 20 pounds. This belief is not unique to me. We are taught from childhood that when we reach a certain goal, our lives will improve. But is it true? Have you ever set a goal for yourself, experienced happiness when you reached it, only to find that the newfound happiness quickly dissipates as if it were never there? In psychology text, this is called "Hedonic Adaptation." We quickly adopt the goal we have reached as the new standard, raising the bar for the next goal. If we once dreamed of a studio apartment, we begin to aspire to a single-family home with a white picket fence once we get it, and then a five-bedroom home, and soon we feel that we cannot possibly manage without a huge balcony or a rooftop for parties, a garden for spices, etc. Money, fame, status, accolades: we can always strive for more of them. Only when we come to understand that happiness is not tied to external factors, but rather lies within us, independent of the size of our house or the size of our bank account, can we break free from the endless cycle of running on the hedonic treadmill.

Each of us has our own "20 pounds"—the one thing we truly and sincerely believe stands between us and pure happiness. When I ask audiences to rate their happiness on a scale of 1 to 10, almost no one rates themselves as a 10. They all believe that happiness is just around the corner, just a little more, not quite yet, only when they have enough money, live in the house of their dreams, find love, have a child, see their daughter get married, retire, finish an Iron Man, run a marathon, or have grandchildren. But in the meantime, life goes on and they are still waiting for that one thing that may or may not happen. The years, however, are not waiting. They will pass by—that's a fact!

So, let's imagine how we would feel if we could be happier today, living the life we dream of right now. We can enjoy everything there is, be freed from this weight (literally—or not), stop running on the hamster wheel, and understand that our happiness does not depend on anything or anyone. It is not found anywhere else except within us, in the gratitude that we have all that we need.

I'm a firm believer in "Yes, and . . ." (a concept that originates from Improv), which encourages us to try and combine different worlds into our lives. It's not about choosing one option or the other, but about choosing one option and the other. There's no contradiction there. So, I try to lose weight and I'm happy with my life.

In this book, I interweave my personal stories with the principles of positive psychology, research, and practical tools that have proven their efficacy. You can also learn about diets (pros and cons), get recipes from my kitchen (if you still decide to go for it . . .), and do some self-work. After all, this book is not really about dieting. So, I recommend answering the questions in each chapter and writing down insights and points for practice. I hope you can adopt some of this very practical philosophy for life and the thought-provoking points it offers.

For Reflection and Self-Work

1. Reflect on what you believe to be the one thing holding you back from true happiness. Identify this as your "20 pounds."

2. Take a moment to consider if you find yourself constantly waiting for something or someone to bring you happiness.
   What is causing this mindset and how can you shift it to focus on finding happiness in the present moment?

For Reflection and Self-Work

3. Think about a past accomplishment or goal that brought you happiness. What was it and how did it make you feel?

4. Reflect on how long that feeling of happiness lasted. Did it dissipate quickly or did it have a lasting impact on your overall well-being?

Recipe

"Yes, and!" Chocolates:
Sweet and Spicy, Delicious and Healthy, Vegan and Easy to Make

Ingredients:

- 1/2 cup of natural coconut butter, free of additives and sugar
- 1/2 cup of cold-pressed coconut oil
- 2 tablespoons of organic cocoa powder
- 1 tablespoon of natural maple syrup
- 1 teaspoon of chili powder
- Walnut pieces
- Cranberries

Instructions:

1. In a medium-sized pot, mix together the coconut butter, coconut oil, cocoa powder, maple syrup, and chili powder.
2. Heat the mixture over low heat, stirring occasionally, until everything is fully melted and combined.
3. Place walnut and cranberry in the bottom of the chocolates mold.
4. Pour the mixture over.
5. Sprinkle a little sea salt on top.
6. Allow the chocolate to cool and solidify in the molds. Once set, remove the chocolate from the molds and enjoy! Keep in the fridge or freezer.

Chapter 2

Life is Meant to Be **Enjoyed!**

If you thought this book was all about strict dieting and punishing yourself, think again! I take great pleasure in all the wonderful things that life has to offer. The joys of the world around us are meant to be relished. Oh, the sheer delight of it all! The experiences that tickle our senses and excite our taste buds! Whether it's indulging in a decadent Michelin-starred meal or savoring the simplicity of street food eaten with our bare hands—I love it all.

A glass of rich, spicy Bordeaux wine makes my heart sing, and a sip of smooth bourbon is like a warm embrace. I'm thrilled by the sensation of the wind in my hair as I drive with the top down in Italy, the notes of old hits from the San Remo Festival filling my ears and the air, heavy with the scent of garlic and white wine. The colorful chaos of a bustling market in Provence, the snap of a fresh baguette, the creamy tang of Brie cheese, and a bottle of wine I just got for only five euros, all enjoyed on a picturesque blanket amid a sea of flowers. The crisp autumn air of New England, the crackle of wood burning in a fireplace, a cold beer shared with friends at a local pub. And of course, there is nothing quite like the warmth of a Friday night Shabbat dinner surrounded by family and loved ones, the aroma of fresh challah bread and the sizzle of lemon rosemary chicken signaling the end of another week and the sweet promise of the weekend to come.

I didn't discover my love for cooking until I was 22 years old and moved out of my parents' home to live in my own apartment in the center of Tel Aviv. It was then that I started experimenting with different types of cuisine, venturing beyond the dishes my mother used to make. I dabbled in craft cocktails and cooking gourmet Italian and French meals, which naturally attracted my friends to come over and provide their unsolicited feedback. I don't recall ever standing in the kitchen with my mother and cooking during my childhood. Baking was and remains out of bounds for me, perhaps because I can't stick to a recipe or any instructions. Even today, improvisation, trial and error remain essential components of my meals. So, every Friday, I would embark on a tour of stores and markets in Tel Aviv, searching for interesting ingredients to experiment with over the weekend. I would buy meat from the butcher shop, vegetables and fruits from a small farm-to-table store, fresh bread from the bakery, fine wines from the liquor store, and, of course, fragrant flowers to adorn the table (though I had to stop using white lilies once I discovered my allergy). My practical, no-nonsense mother used to call me" a feinschmecker"—a connoisseur—"just like your father."

About Hospitality in General, and the Ultimate Seduction Meal in Particular

With no shame or guilt, I discovered that the path to winning the affection of the man of my dreams led directly through his stomach. It was when I prepared the ultimate seduction meal that Dani fell head over heels in love with me, eventually leading to our marriage. Even after more than three decades, this special meal continues to make appearances on significant occasions, albeit with healthier adjustments. It has also been successfully passed down to the younger generation, resulting in multiple marriages. For those interested, the recipes can be found at the end of this chapter.

I must confess that despite my reputation as a

gourmet cook and gracious host, I don't prioritize food itself when choosing a restaurant. It's the atmosphere I'm after. I would rather slip on my red heels, casually drape a black scarf over my shoulders, apply red lipstick and mascara, spritz on some perfume, and cruise in my air-conditioned car to a charming restaurant with crisp white tablecloths and flickering candles. I start with a flawlessly crafted Manhattan cocktail and move on to a bottle of mouth-puckering wine. The truth is the food on the menu doesn't hold much fascination for me. I have delicious food at home. That's why I don't consider myself a foodie—just someone who enjoys life's simple pleasures.

Throughout my culinary journey, I have discovered my love for cooking and experimenting with new recipes. I enjoy challenging myself and modifying my dishes to meet any dietary restrictions. A few years ago, I started hosting cooking classes in my home kitchen. These classes brought together people from all walks of life and of all ages. We would have fun cooking together, like children, and learn how simple it is to bring joy to others through food. In my professional life in business development, I would often invite clients over for cooking classes at my home. These evenings always ended in the dining room, gathered around a long and festive table, savoring the delicious dishes we prepared together, while sharing meaningful conversations, laughter, and happiness.

These classes not only brought joy but also proved to be more successful in securing deals than any marketing or advertising effort I had ever invested in. As we gathered around the kitchen counter, it became clear to me that good food has the power to break down barriers of culture, language, and status. Thanks to my organized approach, even the act of cooking and hosting has become a stress-free and meditative experience. When friends ask what they can bring to a meal, I always reply with a smile, "Just bring comfortable shoes for washing dishes." Ultimately, this approach benefits everyone. However, all these dinner parties, while nourishing for the soul, can be excessive for the body. That's why I've developed the following tips to keep spirits high and my own weight in check:

- Sip on a glass of soda and lemon while everyone is finishing their second cocktail to keep my inhibitions in check and eat mindfully.
- Fill up on a salad to help control portion sizes.
- Always prepare grilled vegetables and healthy sides.
- Eat from the small plate used to serve the first course.

- Limit myself to one serving.
- Enjoy two glasses of wine during the meal, savoring them slowly. Between each drink, have at least two glasses of water.
- Make an effort to forgo dessert on the pretext of clearing the table and escaping quietly to make coffee and tea.
- At the end of the night, send all tempting leftovers that may be hard to resist home with my guests. If I still have some leftovers that I know for sure I'll be tempted to eat tomorrow (like the cream-based smoked salmon dip I served at the beginning of the evening, a liver pâté with blueberry liqueur, or, God forbid, the crème brûlée), I'll douse them with dish soap and throw them in the trash. Forgive me, but it's true.

☛ I Am This and That and That

If you think for one moment that my family enjoys meals like these every day, fear not. Far from it, actually. Growing up, my three children were raised on a diet of chicken fingers, white rice with ketchup, spaghetti and meatballs. But we instilled in them a healthy relationship with food, so they can appreciate both a gourmet meal and fast food. It's all about moderation.

I know it sounds crazy, but my home library contains an equal number of cookbooks and travel magazines, hospitality guides and cocktail recipes, all side-by-side every diet book ever published. From Bordeaux to Atkins, the Michelin Guide to the 4-Hour Diet, my bookshelf embodies the duality of my life. I exist in this dichotomy of enjoyment and discipline, of indulgence and restraint. There is space for both poles in our lives, and I am grateful to embrace them both. (Remember the "Yes, and?")

For Reflection and Self-Work

1. What dualities make up your character?

2. Write down five sentences that consist of "Yes, and . . ."

3. What's the one dish that's totally worth breaking your diet for, guilt-free?

Recipe

The Ultimate Seduction Meal Opening Cocktail: **Kir Royal**

Ingredients:

- Champagne or any sparkling wine
- 1 tablespoon blueberry liqueur or crème de cassis

Instructions:

1. Pour the liqueur into tall champagne glasses.
2. Add chilled champagne or sparkling wine.

Recipe

Appetizer
French Green Salad

Ingredients:

- 2 hearts of Romaine lettuce, washed and dried, torn by hand
- 1/2 cup of walnuts sautéed in olive oil, sprinkled with fresh garlic and salt
- 1/2 cup of quality blue cheese, crumbled into large pieces

Ingredients for the vinaigrette dressing:

- 2 teaspoons of high-quality Dijon mustard
- 2 tablespoons red or white wine vinegar
- Salt and ground black pepper
- 6 tablespoons of olive oil

Instructions:

1. Mix all the ingredients of the dressing, except the oil, which should be added slowly while whisking the mixture with a fork.
2. Combine the lettuce with the vinaigrette.
3. Sprinkle with nuts and cheese.
4. Serve with fresh, warm bread.

Recipe

Main Course

Peppercorn Steak (Steak au Poivre)

Ingredients:

- 2 steaks: New York strip or filet mignon, 2 inches thick
- 2 tablespoons of black peppercorns
- 1 cup heavy whipping cream
- 1/4 cup cognac or brandy
- 1 tablespoon of butter
- 1 tablespoon of oil

Instructions:

1. Place the black peppercorns in a small plastic bag and crush with a mallet or heavy glass.
2. Cover the steak with the pepper mixture and sprinkle with coarse salt.
3. Leave outside the refrigerator for two hours.
4. In a very hot cast iron skillet, melt the butter and heat the oil and fry the steaks for 3-4 minutes on each side.
5. Remove and place on a warm plate.
6. Pour cognac into the pan and scrape the bottom.
7. Cook until the alcohol evaporates, about one minute.
8. Add the juices from the steak plate into the pan.
9. Add cream and bring to a boil, simmer for another minute.
10. Season with more salt and pepper to taste.
11. Return the steaks to the skillet for another minute.
12. Serve hot.

Recipe

Side Dish
Best Ever Mashed Potatoes

Ingredients:

- 4 Yukon Gold potatoes, peeled and cut in half
- 1 tablespoon of butter
- 1/2 cup of hot milk
- Coarse salt and black pepper

Instructions:

1. Cook the potatoes until fork tender.
2. Mash and whisk to a velvety smooth consistency. Add the butter and hot milk.
3. Serve with coarse salt and freshly ground black pepper.

Recipe

Dessert
Vanilla Ice Cream with Hot Chocolate and Whiskey Sauce

Ingredients:

- 4 oz of high-quality dark chocolate (70% cocoa minimum)
- 1 tablespoon whiskey or bourbon
- 2 tablespoons heavy whipping cream
- 2 scoops of vanilla ice cream
- ½ cup of toasted almonds

Instructions:

1. In a glass bowl in the microwave or a small saucepan on the stove, melt the chocolate, whiskey, and heavy cream.
2. Serve a scoop of vanilla ice cream in a beautiful glass and pour the hot chocolate sauce over it.
3. Sprinkle the toasted almonds on top for the perfect finish.

Recipe

Cocktail Black Russian

Ingredients:

- 2 oz of vodka
- 1 oz of Kahlúa or other coffee liqueur
- Ice (optional)

Instructions:

1. Mix the vodka and Kahlúa.
2. Serve over ice or shaken and strained (James Bond style).

It really doesn't get more simple, easy to prepare, or delicious than that. So go ahead, invite me to your wedding.

Chapter 3

Childhood, or "Tami, Just a Few More Bites!"

"Tami!" My mother's voice rings out from the kitchen.

"Just a few more bites, and that's all."

"No, Mom, I've had enough!" I reply, dreading the thought of eating just another bowl of oatmeal.

But my mother is determined. She convinces me to finish so I can enjoy the hidden treasure at the bottom of the bowl: a colorful painting of a cow under a starry sky. It's an illustration I once loved but one that unfortunately reveals itself only after every last bite has been taken.

"Come on, Tami, just five more bites," she says, counting with me. "One, two, three . . ." Our game continues until, with an air of resignation, my mother finally gives up. "By the time you see the cow, I'll see stars!"

Well done, Mom! You did it. From the time I turned six, you no longer had to beg me to eat—I did it beautifully all by myself. And so, gradually and deliberately, the fat cells that would haunt me for eternity began to accumulate.

Tel Aviv, 1962. October arrived with a pleasant breeze, bearing the first hints of autumn. And with it, I entered the world: small, scrappy, and not quite sure what to make of it all. After the first three days, during which my mother was mine alone, they sent me home to meet my redheaded sister. My father was beaming with joy at the arrival of another daughter, and as he looked at the tiny bundle swaddled in a blanket, the setting sun casting a warm glow over my baby hairs, he proclaimed to my mother with a proud smile, "Sara, look—another redhead!"

I was born into a loving family, surrounded by parents, an older sister, a younger brother, grandparents, uncles, aunts, and an abundance of food. My mother was famous for her meatballs, while my grandmothers each excelled in their own specialties—schnitzels and stuffed cabbage, respectively. And every Rosh Hashanah, my father and uncle would engage in a friendly but fierce competition over who got to eat the head of the gefilte fish. "There are hungry children in Africa," I was constantly reminded. "You must finish every last bite."

The day I entered the world, my sister was overjoyed. With the innocence of a one-and-a-half-year-old, her joy only grew as my cheeks rounded out over the years. Not just another redheaded sibling, but a chubby one, too. How fun! My sister and I may look alike, but our personalities couldn't be more different. She was always strong-willed, never giving up on herself or cutting herself slack, disciplined and inflexible when it came to dieting—no cake, no matter how tempting.

"I'm starving," I'd beg. "Let's just have a small slice of the cake Mom made." But she was resolute. "No way." I, on the other hand, have always lived in the gray area, straddling the line between discipline and indulgence. A bite of cake, a sneaky finger in the Nutella jar, a stealthy lick of the knife after spreading peanut butter on the kids' lunch sandwiches, an extra glass of wine. But she, with her iron will and unwavering resolve, never strayed from the path. I can't help but admire her strength and determination, qualities I was unfortunately not blessed with.

Throughout our lives, my sister has been a faithful accomplice on my endless dieting journey. She even became a clinical dietitian, but alas, her sage advice falls on deaf ears (mine). Despite the ups and downs, triumphs and tribulations, we've always remained close, side by side. And although an ocean now separates us, we still maintain our daily ritual of chatting about our meals, our waistlines, and confessing our latest culinary adventures—as if nothing has changed. We have tried every diet under the sun, and to this day, my sister has the upper hand (and the lower weight).

When I was three years old, a sweet baby joined our family who soon slimmed down to a mere wisp. His ribs were visible through his shirt, much to my mother's distress. Deeply attached to the boy, she threw herself into the task of fattening him up: eggs fried in butter with some bread to dip in the yolk, creamy fruit smoothies, thick sweet potato fries, and, of course, ice cream and whipped cream for dessert.

"It's for your brother," she would scold, addressing my sister and me and fueling our jealousy. How did we, two chubby green-eyed girls with fair skin, end up with a younger brother who was tanned, tall, and lean, an athlete, and yes, thin? But before you jump to naughty conclusions, let me just say this: he's the spitting image of my grandfather, a resemblance that only grows stronger with each passing year.

One day in the middle of lunch, which included a perfectly cooked steak and French fries, my brother suddenly laid down his fork and knife and declared that he was no longer hungry. I was shocked, wondering what the connection was between being hungry and finishing a juicy steak.

This perplexity was nothing new for me. For years, I had been scratching my head trying to comprehend how he could leave behind platefuls of delicious food and claim to be "full." Of course, at the end of meals at home, when it was my turn to clear the plates into the sink, my heart wouldn't let the food go to waste and I couldn't resist indulging, adding some extra calories to my daily intake.

You probably already guessed it, but even after 50 years, not much has changed: my brother still eats until he's satisfied. He has never tried dieting and still can't comprehend why his sisters willingly starve themselves. I now realize that our natural tendency to be thin or fat is deeply ingrained, and trying to change it is a lifelong struggle against our own biology. If anything, the three of us siblings are living proof of this reality!

On the Marvels and Miracles of a Kit Kat

Sports were never my thing. While my friends and classmates were busy playing Four Square, climbing trees, or splashing in the community pool, I preferred to curl up with a book. At just five years old, I was already a regular at the local library, where I honed my reading skills alongside my older sister.

I read day and night, devouring every book on the shelves in alphabetical order. I discovered enchanted kingdoms, fairy tales, and the lives of famous composers and painters. I was on my way to becoming cultured and learned, no doubt, but where were the calories burned? The library was just a few blocks away from our house, so my daily walks there didn't exactly count as exercise. Plus, let's be honest, any reading experience is made sweeter with a Kit Kat bar. So, while I became an intelligent and well-read girl (who even wants that?) I longed to be beautiful, thin, and popular. I dreamed of at least being the second runner-up for homecoming queen (the titles of queen and first runner-up had already been claimed).

When I was seven years old, I was so engrossed in a book that I walked straight into the wall of our home's corridor while making my way to the dining room. My mother, a bit worried with the situation, decided it was time for me to enroll in a more productive extracurricular activity. This was in the '60s, when kids weren't offered endless activities like they are now. So, my mother allowed me to choose only one class to focus on. It was always about making choices: between ice cream and a hotdog, between a new swimsuit and a trendy shirt. I stood at a crossroads, torn between piano lessons and ballet. While I longed to play the piano like my father, I couldn't pass up the opportunity for a ballerina's physique. The choice was clear; ballet it was!

The next day, my mother took me to meet the famous ballet teacher, a Russian woman with the tact of a Cossack. She gave me a withering look, carefully sizing me up from my small flat feet to my red hair and round, dimpled face. But her gaze lingered longest on my pudgy belly and spindly legs, and I knew things were not looking up. "Turn around, plié!" she barked, her cutting voice accentuated by her thick Russian accent. "Stand on your toes." And so, I stumbled, turning clumsily.

Without another glance at me, she turned to my mother and growled, "Piano it is! The girl is not built for ballet." It was as if a bucket of cold water had been thrown in my face. My heart sank as I stood there, tears streaming down my cheeks, feeling like the infamous hippo from the movie *Fantasia.* I wished the earth would open up and swallow me whole, just to escape the embarrassment and utter devastation of being told I wasn't good enough. The judgment was swift, brutal, and final. The insult still burns within me, half a century later, a constant reminder that perhaps I'm not quite perfect and my body can't keep up with my mind's desires.

☛ Didn't You Know? Green Apples Are Slimming

And then, during one of our family dinners, my beloved aunt revealed something shocking. Fresh from giving birth to a sweet baby cousin, she had gained a few extra pounds that only seemed to bother her. So, when dessert was served, she politely declined the cake and asked for a simple green apple instead. "I'm on a diet," she declared. "I need to lose weight." It was like a lightbulb moment for me. The idea of a slimming green apple filled me with excitement. "But how?" I wondered. And in that moment, I began my journey of diets that would shape much of my life.

None of my family members could explain why a green apple was considered slimming, and even to this day, nobody seems to know for sure. So, without a clear explanation, I started my quest to understand the secrets of slimming at a young age. It's a journey that many of you probably share with me: a long and exhausting path filled with ups and downs. When I reflect on my life, I don't remember it in terms of calendar months or the movements of the sun and moon. Instead, I remember each period based on the diet I was following at the time.

Summer Saturdays of my childhood were spent at the beach or pool with the family. My father would enjoy a popsicle between cigarettes while my mother would constantly remind him how unhealthy it was. My thin, tanned brother would soak up the sun and play in the waves, while my sister and I would bask in the hot, unfiltered Tel Aviv sun. With no sunblock to be found, my mother attempted to apply a white and embarrassing paste on our noses, but it didn't work. As a result, we ended up looking like two overcooked lobsters, spending our time peeling each other's skin — a ritual that only ended when it was time to leave for the Girl Scouts' weekly activity.

We would only be gone for a few hours before returning home in the evening, starving and sweaty from the scorching sun, ready to eat anything in sight from the fridge or pantry. The familiar phrase "diet starts tomorrow" echoed throughout the house. This ritual continued every Saturday. But things changed after we moved to the United States. The start of the diet was postponed to Mondays instead of Sundays (since the work week starts on Sunday in Israel), and the Saturday night fridge raids were replaced with Sunday restaurant trips with the kids. These trips always ended with me feeling guilty and stuffed, muttering to my husband, "Dani, I can't believe how much I devoured today." It was hardly a display of self-love and compassion.

As time passed, the diets came and went, each with its own set of rules, restrictions, and promises. But one thing remained constant: the ongoing struggle with my self-image and the longing for that elusive perfect body. Despite countless attempts to transform my physical appearance, I realized that the most important transformation needed to happen within my own mindset. The journey to self-acceptance and self-love is just as important, if not more so, than the quest for a smaller waistline.

☛ How Can You Talk Like That? (To Yourself)

When I reflect on those Saturdays spent raiding the fridge and the negative self-talk that accompanied them, I am horrified by the level of self-loathing. When I say to myself, "What a weak cow you are!" I ask myself if I would ever say that to a good friend. Of course not! I would say something like, "So what if you ate that cake? It's delicious and comforting," or "You had a tough day; it's OK, treat yourself."

We are capable of having so much empathy for strangers but none for ourselves. We talk to ourselves in a way that we would never talk to the people we love. Why? Because that's how we were brought up. We were probably judged, reprimanded, and burdened with expectations by our parents or other adults in our lives. As a result, we are the ones doing it to ourselves today.

Kristin Neff, a leading expert on compassion, defines self-compassion as, "Instead of mercilessly judging and criticizing yourself for various inadequacies or shortcomings, self-compassion means you are kind and understanding when confronted with personal failings after all, who ever said you were supposed to be perfect?"(1)

Life isn't always going to go the way we want. We will encounter challenges, make mistakes, face limitations, and forget our priorities and resolutions. This is a common human experience. The more we accept and understand this reality, the more we can show compassion towards ourselves and others.

Neff clarifies, "Self-compassion is also very different from self-indulgence. Many people say they are reluctant to be self-compassionate because they're afraid they would let themselves get away with anything. 'I'm stressed out today, so to be kind to myself, I'll just watch TV all day and eat a quart of ice cream.' This, however, is self-indulgence rather than self-compassion."

In her book *Self-Compassion,* Neff provides us with three key principles to help us cultivate self-compassion:

- Treat ourselves kindly instead of harshly.
- See ourselves as part of the larger human experience.
  Nobody is perfect.
- Practice mindfulness—observe situations objectively without judgment.

Dr. Tal Ben-Shahar, my esteemed teacher and mentor, frequently speaks of the "permission to be human" as a crucial aspect of emotional well-being and happiness. He emphasizes the importance of acknowledging that it's okay to fail, to experience pain, sadness, frustration, or any other painful emotion. After all, no one lives up to the carefully curated lives they present on Facebook or Instagram. The reality is that those seemingly perfect individuals don't exist; they don't look that great, bake perfect sourdough bread, or receive endless love from their children. The truth is, when we fall, stumble, and indulge in a late-night binge of buttered baguette and half a bottle of wine, we're not alone. Let's not make things worse by also punishing ourselves for the extra pound or two and the inevitable stomachache. Embracing our humanity means accepting our flaws and imperfections, and recognizing that we're part of a larger human experience.

Diets aside, how often do we belittle ourselves in general? Criticizing and judging without a shred of mercy? Let's put a stop to that. Each time that voice in our heads tuts and we suddenly feel unworthy, mean, unsuccessful, and ugly, let's ask ourselves how we would treat a cherished friend in that moment. Let's extend ourselves the same love and a comforting embrace. After all, as Eleanor Roosevelt once said, "Friendship with oneself is all-important because without it one cannot be friends with anybody else in the world." As a reminder, I often repeat the following to myself, which helps to put things into perspective: "When I'm 80 years old and looking back, will any of this really matter?"

For Reflection and Self-Work

1. Do you treat yourself with kindness and empathy in your self-talk?

2. What phrases do you commonly use in your self-talk? Would you say these to a loved one?

3. How can you change your negative self-talk habits?

4. What affirmations or statements help you gain perspective?

Recipe

Mom's Fried **Meatballs**

These are the meatballs my mother once had to beg me to eat. Now, I can't resist eating them straight from the pan, justifying it with her words, "Eat something, Tamile, you've had a rough day."

Ingredients:

- 2 lbs. ground beef
- 2 eggs
- 1 small potato, peeled and finely grated
- 1 small onion, finely grated
- Salt and pepper, to taste
- 1/2 cup club soda
- 1 cup breadcrumbs for mixing
- 1 cup breadcrumbs for coating
- Oil for frying

Recipe

Mom's Fried **Meatballs.**

Instructions:

1. In a large mixing bowl, combine the ground beef, eggs, grated potato, grated onion, salt, pepper, club soda, and 1 cup of breadcrumbs. Mix well until the mixture forms a consistent texture.
2. Shape the mixture into large meatballs, each about 2 inches in diameter. Gently flatten each ball.
3. Place the remaining cup of breadcrumbs in a shallow dish. Roll each meatball in the breadcrumbs until it's evenly coated.
4. Heat oil in a large frying pan over high heat. Add the meatballs and fry until golden brown on both sides. Then reduce the heat to medium-low and continue cooking until the meatballs are fully cooked through and no longer pink in the center (about 5 minutes on each side).
5. Transfer the cooked meatballs to a plate lined with paper towels to drain any excess oil.
6. Serve hot and enjoy!

Chapter 4

A Diet That Forbids **an Apple?**

I recall a particularly cold Saturday in the heart of winter. After a hearty stew and my parents' ritual afternoon nap, some family friends dropped by for coffee and cake. My brother quickly ran off to play, while my sister and I joined the adults in the garden, pretending to be engrossed in our books while half-listening to their animated chatter. As the conversation unfolded, I overheard one friend—who had surprisingly declined the cake but requested heavy cream in his coffee sharing a secret he'd discovered during a recent trip abroad. "You won't believe the latest diet craze in America," he began. "Everyone's going nuts over it and shedding pounds like never before." My sister and I exchanged a glance, our interest piqued, and subtly tuned in to learn more. "You start the day with two eggs fried in butter, Brie cheese, and cream in your coffee," our family friend enlightened my wide-eyed father. "Then it's steaks, cheeses, and whipped cream for dessert. Vegetables and fruits are a no-go, and it only allows for a bit of lettuce after a couple of weeks."

Could this be true? Had I misunderstood? What happened to my aunt's revered green apple? I was sold at the mere mention of butter and Brie for breakfast. My sister and I exchanged a knowing look, silently agreeing that we had stumbled upon the diet of our dreams. For those unfamiliar with diet trends, let me introduce you to the game-changing Atkins diet of the 1970s. This revolutionary diet (2), which championed protein and fat over carbohydrates, caused quite a stir and paved the way for diets like paleo, ketogenic, South Beach, and more. And yes, as incredulous as it may sound, my father's friend's description was right on the money. I was hooked.

The next morning, my sister and I woke up early, eager to embark on this new American trend. We were confident that our parents would share our enthusiasm for this culinary adventure, but we were met with firm opposition from our mother. "Not everything adults do is suitable for you, young ladies. The answer is no!" I nudged my sister under the table and, after a river of tears, threats to run away from home, and earnest pleas, my mother finally caved in. "But only for one week, no more." With a sense of triumph, we quickly fried eggs in butter, enjoyed them with cream cheese, relished hot chocolate with half-and-half (no sugar), and headed off to school feeling light as feathers (or at least as light as we hoped to become!). During our mid-morning break, while our classmates munched on hearty subs, my sister and I devoured some hard-boiled eggs. However, the nausea wasn't far behind. By the end of the exhausting school day, we dragged ourselves up the hill to our house, our heads spinning and stomachs churning. Upon arriving home, we immediately sat down to celebrate with a massive steak, devoid of any greens or potatoes. Can this really be considered dinner? And what's for dessert? Exhausted, we collapsed onto our beds in our shared room, locked eyes, and conceded that perhaps the American diet wasn't the miracle we had imagined. After a few more hours of desperately clinging to our dignity, the diet became unbearable. We gave up, pleading with our mother for some toast and a vegetable, yes, a vegetable, and of course, a green apple.

"Why do we put ourselves through this?" I often contemplate, as I once again embark on a new low-carb, high-fat diet, fueled by glossy promises and the desperate hope that this time, things will be different. Isn't that the definition of insanity, as Albert Einstein once pointed out? Repeating the same actions while expecting different results? Yet, here I am again, this time placing all of my hopes on the ketogenic diet, touted as the new miracle solution for weight loss. Seduced by my sister's success—she recently shed her excess pounds and joined the "lean" majority of our three-sibling family (yes, two out of three of us are now on the slimmer side)—I overlook our fundamental differences in personality and surrender myself to the allure of this strict regimen. Predictably, the outcome remains unchanged: I give in to temptation, sneaking a bite here, taking a sip there, disrupting the fragile state of ketosis that supposedly triggers weight loss. The market is flooded with diets of this kind, each with its own unique twist: low-carb, high-fat from animal products, limited vegetable options, or even more challenging variations. It all depends on our personal beliefs about what is considered healthy and what is not. But these diets can work . . . under certain conditions.

- Why try: Effortless weight loss, no hunger, minimal kitchen work, and travel-friendly.
- Why not try: Inflexible and unforgiving, unappetizing (at least to me), with limited fruit and vegetable

options, monotonous, and lacking variety.

☛ The Gap Between Scientific Research and "Me-search"

Research and statistics have their place, but what truly matters is understanding ourselves, our tendencies, and our aspirations for our lifestyle. Dr. Tal Ben-Shahar discusses the distinction between research and "me-search." Studies confirm that low-carb, high-fat diets can indeed lead to significant weight loss. Science explains this through intricate concepts like ketosis and insulin resistance, but I'm not an expert in biology or chemistry. I simply know myself. Over time, I have figured out what works (and doesn't work) for me. And here's my takeaway: I'm not obsessed with perfection. I strive for "good enough." Moderation is my motto. What's the harm in having a slice of challah on Shabbat or a glass of wine? Sure, I could wrap a burger in a lettuce leaf, but secretly, I would be nibbling on the buns that I discreetly saved earlier. So what? These diets are not for me. Just one slice of challah would take me out of ketosis immediately, and I would have to start all over again, with all the fat settling back exactly where I'm trying to get rid of it. These diets cater to the perfectionists among us, but for me, a little bit of everything works just fine.

Yet, this book is not about diets. So, how does all of this relate to life as a whole, you might wonder? In my opinion—and I acknowledge that many may disagree — perfectionism is a double-edged sword. It paralyzes us and isolates us from others. It's challenging to be a perfectionist, to raise one, to be raised by one, or to be in a relationship with one. And for someone like me, adhering to a perfectionist diet is equally daunting. Therefore, for those who see the world in black and white, who can resist the tempting smell of freshly baked cake, who have the discipline to travel to Italy and turn down a hearty bowl of spaghetti, this diet might be a good fit (and I even offer an enticing, compliant recipe). But for the rest of us, the search continues.

For Reflection and Self-Work

1. Do you lean more towards being a perfectionist or do you adopt the "good enough" way of life?

2. Which aspects of your life reveal your perfectionist tendencies?

3. How can you apply a "good enough" approach in various areas of your life?

Recipe

Gravlax with **Dill-Cream Sauce**

Ingredients:

For the Gravlax:

- 1 fresh salmon fillet
- 1/2 cup sugar and 1/2 cup kosher salt (or 1 cup of salt if you're strictly adhering to the keto diet)
- Black peppercorns
- 1 shot of vodka
- 3 tablespoons of chopped dill

For the Sauce:

- 1/2 cup of sour cream
- 1 tablespoon of mayonnaise
- 1 clove of garlic, chopped
- Chopped dill
- 1 grated hard-boiled egg
- Capers
- 1 Chopped onion

Recipe

Gravlax with **Dill-Cream Sauce**

Instructions:

1. Mix the salt (and sugar if chosen), pepper, vodka, and chopped dill in a bowl.
2. Place the salmon fillet on a sheet of plastic wrap.
3. Cut the salmon in half. Cover one piece with the salt mixture, then lay the other half of the salmon on top like a sandwich and wrap it tightly.
4. Transfer the wrapped salmon into a pan, then cover it with a baking sheet. Weigh down the baking sheet with heavy objects, such as cans.
5. Allow the salmon to cure for 2–3 days in the fridge, depending on your preference.
6. Unwrap the salmon, rinse it thoroughly, pat it dry with a paper towel, and cut it diagonally into thin slices.
7. For the sauce, combine the sour cream, mayonnaise, chopped garlic, and dill.
8. Serve the sliced gravlax alongside the dill-cream sauce, garnished with grated hard-boiled egg, capers, and chopped onion.

Enjoy!

Chapter 5

My Blissful Teenage Years (Not So Much . . .)

And so, I entered my teenage years. I joined the local Girl Scouts, hoping to embrace the adventures of camping trips and summer camps, but I always felt homesick, like I didn't fit in. Even at 18, during my military basic training, I longed for the familiarity and comfort of home. I struggled to connect with my peers, often feeling like I didn't belong. Despite having many girlfriends and being known for my humor and wit, I found myself drawn to the boys. I valued my friendships with them, but when it came to romantic beachside evenings, it seemed like only the conventionally attractive girls were chosen. On summer vacation hikes, I would lag behind with a red face, cursing the ease with which the other girls effortlessly climbed the rocks while I struggled. During dance parties, I sought solace in conversations with other wallflowers, pretending not to be bothered that the boys had already paired up with their graceful, flirtatious partners. Oh, how I longed to be one of those girls!

The pinnacle of these teenage embarrassments was the weekend trip to the beach. We'd hop on the bus, our trusty tote bags and beach cover-ups in tow, ready to hit the sand at the beach across from the old Sheraton hotel in Tel Aviv. Upon arrival, the boys would already be there, stirring up a lively atmosphere with their flirtatious laughter and adolescent energy. Meanwhile, the girls had gracefully removed their beach cover-ups, revealing bronzed skin glistening with tanning oil that provided no sun protection. They jumped in the water, giggled during games of paddleball, and whispered secrets to each other. I felt like an outsider in this scene.

Soon enough, the moment of truth would arrive—it was time to strip down to my own full-body bathing suit. But there was a ritual to follow. First, you had to remove your shorts, then sit down on the towel, and before anyone could see you from an unflattering angle, quickly and discreetly lie down flat on your back to carefully peel off the T-shirt while horizontal. The key was to execute all of this with practiced nonchalance. And there I was, in my bathing suit, lying on my back, stomach sucked in as far as it would go, barely breathing, yet striving to look like a bombshell.

Of course, it was difficult to engage in conversation in such a state, especially when you could hardly draw breath. But, when you're young, anything seems possible. The rules were clear: stand or lie down, but never sit in a bathing suit! I wasn't alone in this struggle, and surrounded by other girls who also battled with body image. So overall, this feeling of insecurity was disturbingly normal.

Years passed, and one day I shared my "lying or standing" rule with my best friend. Her eyes widened in disbelief as she asked, "What? Lying down on the beach? Are you out of your mind?" As it turned out, not all women shared my viewpoint. "We flat-chested girls," she said, "never dared to lie down—only to stand or sit!" That's when I realized that everyone brings their own insecurities to the game. We suffer the long-term damage of teenage body image for many years later, with only a few of us who got away without a scratch.

If It Weren't Funny, It'd Be Sad

These teenage years were filled with an array of diets. I tried them all, in relentless pursuit of the ideal flat tummy and the elusive goal of constant slimness. Every other week, a new fad diet took the spotlight: Rabin diet, the grapefruit diet, the bread diet, and, of course, the infamous cabbage soup diet. I didn't miss a single one.

Days were filled with nothing but cucumbers and plain non-fat yogurt, strong black coffee, and endless chewing of gum on an empty stomach, which resulted in serious ulcer pain. The grapefruit diet only made matters worse, aggravating the issues from the previous diet. The Rabin diet was utter madness: eating only one type of food each day for five days and losing four pounds, only to gain five pounds the following week. The bread diet worked, as long as you followed it correctly. That meant six slices of light bread a day topped with a smidgen of low-fat cottage cheese, not like my classmate who indulged in eight challah rolls slathered with butter and was shocked to see her weight increase by an extra seven pounds by Saturday.

But let's face it. Looking back at those old photos now, it's somewhat melancholic. What was I even thinking, subjecting myself to such pressure to be thin? With my long legs and adorable dimple, I should have been enjoying my youth and hitting the dance floor. Chances are my friends didn't spend a single second worrying about whether I looked fat or thin after a day at the beach. Who cares, right? We all hold ourselves back from living our best lives and pursuing what truly makes us happy because we're afraid of what others might say or think.

Well, I've got some news for you: they won't say anything. And five minutes after everyone goes back to their own lives, they won't even be thinking about me. I certainly don't come home from the beach and start critiquing other people's appearances. My life is too interesting to focus on anything else as soon as I return to it. Recognizing this may be challenging, but it is also incredibly liberating. We're all wrapped up in our own concerns, and if someone is nosy enough to waste their time pondering about my life instead of their own then good for them! The topic of body image is curious, isn't it? It's fascinating how the reflection in the mirror can be so different from the image we hold in our minds. I know of curvaceous women and men who radiate sexiness, confidence, and charisma, and are simply stunning. Take Queen Latifah, for instance. Every time I see her on the screen, I can't help but admire her. I don't see what society would call flaws. I just see a beautiful, full-bodied woman. Then there are my friends who suffer from the opposite syndrome. They're thin in their minds and big in imagination. They were slim as children, but things have changed over the years, and they still haven't adjusted. They walk down the street, catch a glimpse of their grandmother staring back at them from a store window, and can't believe it's their own reflection. They try on a size 2 in a store and are shocked when they can't even get the pants past their knees. Perhaps they are happier that way. Who knows? But here's something I can say for sure: there is no correlation between the image in the mirror and the one in our heads. If only I had the wisdom I possess today back then. If only I could have had the perspective that I have now . . .

The Quote to Frame or Print on a T-Shirt

Dr. Haim Shapira, an Israeli philosopher and speaker, referenced in one of his lectures, a quote from Nobel Prize–winning psychologist Daniel Kahneman. The quote struck a chord with me and has helped refine my understanding of the idea of perspective: "Nothing in life is as important as you think it is, while you are thinking about it." This idea marked a turning point for me.

As a young girl, my chief concern was being thin and having a flat stomach. I was so preoccupied with my appearance, what I was wearing, and my physical attributes—height, weight—that they seemed as important to me as the security situation in Israel or my future career. Now, with the passage of time and a shift in perspective, I understand these concerns were less significant than I believed then. Since this is not a book about diets, let's consider how we can apply this newfound insight in our daily lives.

Happiness expert Professor Sonja Lyubomirsky suggests that maintaining a healthy perspective is one of the key traits of happy people (3). Just as in the chapter on love and self-compassion, perspective plays a crucial role here too. So, how do we put this into practice? My advice is to keep this powerful statement—"Nothing in life is as important as you think it is, while you are thinking about it" as a constant reminder. Set it as your phone's lock screen, print it out and frame it, embroider it onto a shirt if you want! When we feel overwhelmed, as if something terrible has happened, or that we must fight tooth and nail for something, it's essential to take a step back, zoom out, gain perspective, and remind ourselves of this all-encompassing truth. Gaining perspective begins with being mindful and aware.

☛ Harness Your Strengths, Manage Your Weaknesses

Intuitively, I reached another conclusion when I was very young, but only connected it years later as a key principle of positive psychology. The idea is to focus on our strengths rather than trying to fix our weaknesses. There's always something positive in each of us and every situation, so why not highlight it? This doesn't mean ignoring our weaknesses or less-appealing aspects, but rather acknowledging them without letting them dominate the experience.

Later in my teens and early twenties, I understood that I'd be wiser to emphasize my beautiful eyes with a streak of blue eyeliner instead of, say, wearing a tight shirt that accentuated my less-flattering features. A unique haircut suits me much better than a bikini. There's always something to work with and something to emphasize. In any situation, we can always focus on the good. We don't deny reality or bury our heads in the sand; we concentrate on the positive, the solutions instead of problems and strengths instead of weaknesses. As Peter Drucker, an American thinker and business consultant, said, "It's the abilities, not the disabilities, that count."

The thing is, most of us struggle when it comes to identifying our strengths. Ask us to list our weaknesses, problems, and shortcomings, and we could give you an endless list in minutes. However, when it comes to highlighting our strengths, what we're good at, and what's beautiful about us, it's a completely different story. It's challenging and requires time and effort.

That's because we've been taught to be modest, not to brag. But here's the thing, research shows that focusing solely on our weaknesses and trying to fix them will only bring us to mediocrity at best. To reach excellence and achieve great things, we need to focus on and strengthen our strengths. Of course, we shouldn't ignore our weaknesses, but we should work to manage them so they don't prevent us from reaching our full potential.

For Reflection and Self-Work

1. What are your top ten strengths? What are you good at? What comes naturally to you? Consider taking online strength tests like the VIA Strengths Test or Clifton StrengthsFinder.

For Reflection and Self-Work

2. What are some of your best physical and personal traits?

3. Which weaknesses or flaws have you been focusing on, and how can you reduce their impact to achieve excellence?

4. What once seemed essential to you but now you realize is not as important as you once thought?

Recipe

Low-Calorie Cucumber and Yogurt Salad

(tried it for a week once . . .)

Ingredients:

- Cucumbers
- Non-fat plain yogurt
- Chives

That's it!

Instructions:

1. Mix and season with salt and pepper to taste.
2. If you have some leftover calories from your daily 500 allowance, indulge with a teaspoon of extra virgin olive oil.

Chapter 6

Detoxifying My Body (and Bank Account)

I've lost count of the number of healers and detox gurus to whom I've given my hard-earned money and, more importantly, my hope and faith. But one stands out in particular. A few years ago, I bumped into an old friend I hadn't seen in weeks. She looked amazing—slimmer, radiant, and with a distant, blissful look in her eyes. As we settled in the kitchen, I raised a glass to celebrate our reunion, but she declined with a smile and chose herbal tea instead. I, on the other hand, stuck to my salt-rimmed margarita, but couldn't help feeling that I would soon need to join her on the tea train if I wanted to keep up with her weight loss. "What's your secret?" I asked, a mix of envy and curiosity. "I did a detox with a special doctor," she casually replied.

A detox? I hadn't tried one yet, but I was immediately convinced. I begged her for the name of this highly sought-after "doctor" and somehow managed to secure an appointment with him for the very next day (in hindsight, I should have seen the red flags). Filled with excitement and hope, I practically skipped out of the office and weaved through traffic to arrive at the clinic early. I walked in, brimming with anticipation. The receptionist greeted me and conducted a thorough interview that included questions and measurements. After she left the room, the doctor entered—handsome and charismatic, the promised healer, the detoxification Messiah himself. He sat down in front of me and showed genuine interest and empathy as he inquired about my life, my desires, and all the diets that had failed me. It felt like he understood my soul and knew where I had gone astray. I almost wanted to hug him in gratitude for finally getting to the heart of who I was.

He listened intently to my dietary woes and, without batting an eye, pinpointed the root of my problem—the toxins and poisons that had accumulated in my body and were now stored deep in my fat cells. Of course, I agreed wholeheartedly, given my previous attempts at dieting with minimal success. What a revelation! How could I have not thought of this before? And with that, he revealed the solution to my problem—the detoxification method that he sold, and no doubt made a fortune from. I was a fool, but I was also "toxic," and now I had the chance to be cured.

With high hopes and grand expectations, I eagerly awaited the arrival of my new miracle solution. And boy, did it come loaded. Not only did I purchase the most premium package, but I also opted in for every extra they offered—every single one! The powders, the potions, the supplements, the meetings, and even the fasts (yes, they charged a handsome sum for nothing but hunger)—I bought it all. And to top it off, I threw in a couple of creams to combat potential wrinkles, figuring the expected weight loss would leave some loose skin. All with express delivery, of course. I couldn't wait to start my journey to the promised land of weight loss and rejuvenation.

And then, as luck would have it, the package arrived just in time for the holiday season. And what a season it was! Endless parties and meals, not to mention my dear friend Sara visiting from Norway—a trip we had planned for years. I stayed firm in my belief, however, that a glass of green sludge and a couple of fasting days wouldn't spoil our fun. After all, our friendship was resilient enough to endure a little detox, right?

So, I plunged in, drinking my potions, feeling so good as I effortlessly shed 15 pounds, along with a few good friends whom I attempted to recruit into the pyramid scheme, and half of my hair. A year later, all the weight returned, my friends (somewhat reluctantly) came back, and it seemed the toxins I had so fervently tried to banish had quietly snuck their way back into my life.

Years have passed since then, and while I've experimented with other detoxification programs and juice fasts, I never revisited that mysterious blend of ingredients I could barely pronounce. The hair loss and questionable decisions I made during that time taught me a valuable lesson or at least, I'd like to believe so.

What I Learned (the Hard Way)

What did I truly learn from all this? Probably not as much as I should have. Just a few months ago, I ordered a fast-mimicking kit that an acupuncturist highly recommended. "It's from Italy," she informed me. "Delicious, simple, and the results are guaranteed." Naturally, being someone who doesn't argue with experts, I promptly purchased it. If only I could shed a half pound for every dollar I spent. But I digress.

The miraculous kit arrived, complete with instructions to eat a granola bar and olives in the morning, and tomato or mushroom powder soup (Italian, of course) with seven almonds at noon and in the evening. The kit claimed that these foods slipped under the body's detection radar, making the body think it was fasting when it was actually not. My body, however, seemed to comprehend quite well that it was indeed eating.

I completed the kit twice, lost five pounds, and regained them at the first dinner party where I was permitted to eat again. I even stashed a box of bars in the fridge, counting it as fasting, but that's a tale for another time.

So what's the deal with detoxification? To me, it seems more logical to prevent the accumulation of toxins in the first place, rather than attempting to cleanse them later. Our unhealthy habits like smoking, drinking, eating sugar, processed foods, and chemicals have a lasting impact on our bodies, leading to diseases and obesity. Instead of just relying on detoxification methods, we should focus on breaking these harmful habits to prevent further damage. Adopting new habits is one thing, but the real challenge lies in breaking old habits—and that's where the true work begins.

☛ The Broken Promise of Willpower

Let's get straight to the point: willpower doesn't cut it. It's not our fault that we find it hard to make changes, and it's not because of a lack of willpower or character.

In fact, research shows that willpower is a finite resource that dwindles as the day progresses (4). So why do we still manage to rise every morning to shower, brew coffee, or solve a puzzle? It's not willpower; it's because these activities have morphed into habits.

Habits develop through repeated actions that eventually become automatic. The field of neuroplasticity explores how our brain can change and adapt, and it's now widely accepted that our mind retains flexibility until our final breath. If we consistently make certain actions habitual, they forge new connections in the brain, new pathways. Like a river that has coursed the same path for years, it ultimately carves a deep groove where the water flows naturally—that's the power of habit.

☛ But How?

Various theories exist regarding the time required to establish a habit, but from personal experience, it took me many years to cultivate a habit of walking or exercising. I'd position my sneakers next to the bed, only to step over them instead. On the other hand, I managed to successfully modify some of my dietary habits, some rapidly and others gradually. Awareness is key, but I'm a slow learner—what can I say?

Getting rid of old habits is an entirely different challenge, especially when they yield pleasure, like coupling a cigarette with coffee or gravitating towards the fridge when feeling anxious. But don't lose heart! Consistent reminders and prompts can work wonders.

In all facets of our lives, be it relationships (arrange a weekly date, have a family Zoom call every Friday evening), diet (drink two glasses of water in the morning, opt for a green salad for lunch, savor an espresso for dessert), exercise (commit to walking with a friend twice a week, schedule Zumba classes), or happiness (meditate each morning post-coffee, note down in a gratitude journal every evening before bed, reserve two hours every week just for yourself), the more we prioritize and invest in habit formation, the more we can affect the desired change, without leaning on the unreliable crutch of willpower.

Here are some habits I've cultivated over the years that contribute to my overall well-being and happiness:

- Start the day with a cup of coffee and some quiet time outdoors, appreciating the splendor of nature—this is my meditation.
- Always carry a water bottle with me, ensuring I

drink up to a gallon by day's end.

- Start every meal with a nutritious green salad.
- Take a moment to welcome the weekend by lighting a candle on Friday night, savoring a glass of wine, and expressing gratitude.
- Reflect on five things I'm thankful for each night before sleep.
- Start the day on a positive note by hugging my husband and children (if they're around).
- Indulge in a well-deserved siesta on Saturday afternoons.
- Let loose and sing at the top of my lungs in the car.
- Limit excessive exposure to news.
- Always come prepared with two books for every flight.
- And, last but not least, never forget to enjoy a good, hearty laugh.

For Reflection and Self-Work

1. What healthy and happy habits have you established in your life?

2. What new habits would you like to adopt?

3. What steps can you take to establish these habits?

For Reflection and Self-Work

4. What habits do you want to break?

5. What strategies can you use to break these habits?

Recipe

Detoxifying Salad

For those who wish to cleanse their bodies without relying on strange and unpronounceable potions.

Ingredients:

- 1 fresh fennel bulb, with stalks removed
- A handful of arugula
- A handful of chopped cilantro
- A handful of chopped parsley
- A handful of chopped mint
- A handful of chopped basil
- Sunflower seeds

Optional: pomegranate seeds

Lemon Dressing Ingredients:

- Juice of 2 lemons
- 2 tablespoons of cold-pressed organic olive oil
- 1 clove of minced garlic
- Pinch of pink Himalayan salt, to taste

Recipe

Detoxifying Salad

Instructions:

1. Slice the fennel into thin strips and set aside.
2. In a mixing bowl, combine the chopped cilantro, parsley, mint, and basil.
3. In a separate small bowl, mix the lemon juice, minced garlic, and salt for the dressing. Slowly add the olive oil, whisking until well combined.
4. Combine the fennel and herbs in a large salad bowl. Add the sunflower seeds and optional pomegranate seeds.
5. Drizzle the lemon dressing over the salad and gently toss to combine.
6. Serve the detoxifying salad alongside plain basmati rice, cooked without spices or oil. Enjoy!

Chapter 7

My Undergraduate Years, or the Rice Diet

In all honesty, I had always dreamed of being a flight attendant for El Al, Israel's premier airline. I would have even taken a job as a reservations agent, but alas, I wasn't accepted. My father, however, wasn't thrilled about this career choice and persuaded me to pursue economics at university instead. So, with my obligatory military service due to end in January and university set to begin in October, I seized the opportunity to be released three months early and started my studies at Tel Aviv University.

The day I was discharged from the army, which coincidentally was my 20th birthday, I experienced a sense of happiness, liberation, and freedom like never before. I felt like a butterfly spreading its wings and embarking on a new life. My commanders in the army were equally relieved to see me finally depart, and thus concluded my short but still excessively long chapter in military service.

While my recently discharged friends were globe-trotting as backpackers, the Levin parents envisioned a different path for their offspring. I may not have considered myself enlightened after a six-month camping expedition, but I could now proudly identify myself as an economics student at Tel Aviv University, which felt quite impressive. And I reveled in my newfound freedom. I lived at home with my parents, drove to university every day in my reliable 1965 Peugeot 403 (which had a tendency to break down at almost every turn), and yes, I was happy. My major was engaging, and I didn't mind putting in the effort for my studies. In fact, compared to the army, those days felt carefree and full of potential. I enjoyed them . . . almost. Now that I was free from my uniform, I could dress how I wanted, style my hair, turn heads in the cafeteria, and, of course, start dieting again.

☛ Tel Aviv 35 Years Ago, and I'm Searching for Brown Rice

During exams, my classmates and I would huddle together, fueled by cigarettes and food—an excessive amount of food. But just prior to a major economics exam, my dear aunt (the one with the green apple) introduced me to a new diet: the rice diet! One that only permitted brown or basmati rice and a soy sauce substitute called tamari. This was over 35 years ago, when health food stores were few and far between in Tel Aviv and brown rice and soy sauce, let alone their substitutes, were pricey and rare delicacies. But nothing could deter me and my pursuit of slimness. And with that, I discreetly slipped away from my study group one afternoon for a few hours and combed the streets of Tel Aviv until I sourced the required ingredients at a small natural foods store. For four days, I subsisted on bowls of brown rice cooked in water (no salt, of course) and the fancy soy substitute —oh, and unlimited water and tea. On the fourth day, the diet permitted some veggies, but by then, I'd lost my zest for life, the joy of companionship, and the ability to focus. I think I added a zucchini or two before the big test, just for good measure.

The Economics 101 exam was a disaster waiting to happen, even on a full stomach, so you can imagine the calamity that unfolded with an empty stomach and a foggy mind. When grades were posted later that week, I, with shaky legs, pushed through the throngs of students to read the list, having already decided to hit the campus pub with my classmates that evening, a decision further cemented by my failing grade of 56. It was time to drown my first-term sorrows with a beer and pizza and prepare for the next term.

Recently, I revisited the rice diet and was surprised to find that it is still popular, ranking high on Google. Its methods have remained unchanged over the years. I can't quite explain it, but I felt a sudden urge to try it again. To my surprise, I even lost a pound or two. However, the true pleasure came from the flood of memories that accompanied the first bite of tamari-soaked rice. The distinct aroma transported me back to my university days, a time of pure joy, new beginnings, and complete freedom. I really miss those days. I wish I could relive them. But that was over 35 years ago. Now, I'm married, burdened with a mortgage and other responsibilities, and living in a different world. I can't go back in time, but I can evoke those nostalgic feelings in the present with just a bite. I found myself contemplating what made those happy times in my life so special and how I could reintroduce some of that happiness into my life today.

Happiness Awaits Us at Every Turn

What I did instinctively is called "Appreciative Inquiry" in professional psychology circles, a process conceived in the 1980s by organizational consultant and Case Western Reserve University professor, David

Cooperrider (5). It strives to catalyze positive change in organizations by using the principles of positive psychology. It questions: What is functioning well in the organization? When was it performing better? What contributed to its better performance? What are the organization's strengths? From this, it infers: What actions can bring about the desired change? The emphasis is on solutions and effective practices. Much like organizations, our personal lives can also prosper from retrospection in an appreciative manner, focusing on the positives rather than solely on problems and difficulties.

So, I did just that and embarked on a self-discovery journey. And what did I uncover? I came across a wealth of memories from my younger years, brimming with enthusiasm and awe. It was a period when everything was fascinating and nothing seemed impossible. Certainly, there were challenges. I remember the grueling study sessions from dawn till dusk, and the longing I felt as I trudged down the streets on my way to a study group at a friend's house, wishing I could join the rest of the world at cafés and parties. But occasional hardships aside, the future was expansive, filled with boundless possibilities.

Years have since passed, and I'm now happily married with three grown children, living a comfortable, if somewhat predictable, life. While there may not be much excitement or novelty in my day-to-day routine, I yearned to rekindle that sense of anticipation and wonder. So, my husband and I made a bold decision: we retired from the family business, packed our bags, and set off on a journey.

For three months, we roamed the New York and New Jersey area, embracing the unknown. And what an adventure it was! We met the warmest people who welcomed us into their lives, resided in a charming cabin nestled among the trees with their fiery red leaves, explored the city, and reconnected with our children who live in New York without the usual parental pressures. We relished delicious Shabbat dinners with our kids, took in an opera at the Metropolitan, and rediscovered the thrill of adventure. Slowly but surely, the excitement returned, along with a newfound sense of youth and freedom.

I'm not suggesting that everyone should or even can pack their bags and traverse the globe. But there are countless ways to tap into that sense of wonder and excitement, no matter your age, budget, or circumstances. Whether it's an annual road trip with your best friend, a picnic in the park, learning a new skill, or simply savoring the scent of lavender in your herb garden on a warm summer night, the possibilities are endless. There is always an opportunity to recapture the essence of our past experiences and integrate them into our present lives. The key is to remain open and receptive to those small moments that can spark joy, inspire change, and ultimately, enrich our lives.

For Reflection and Self-Work

1. Reflect on a time in your life when joy overflowed and radiated from every moment. What made it such a happy experience?

2. How can you infuse a little of that magic into your present reality?

3. Imagine the sky's the limit—what do you believe is within your reach?

Recipe

Green Rice to the **Rescue!**

Ingredients:

- 2 cups of brown or basmati rice
- 3 cups boiling water (for basmati) or 4 cups boiling water (for brown rice)
- 2 cloves of garlic, peeled
- 3 celery stalks, finely chopped
- A bunch of cilantro
- A bunch of mint
- A bunch of parsley
- Grated rind from half a lemon

Instructions:

1. Combine rice, water, garlic, and a pinch of salt in a pot.
2. Cook on low heat for 20 minutes and then turn off heat, leaving the pot closed for another 10 minutes.
3. Fluff the rice with a fork.
4. Finely chop all herbs and mix with the rice just before serving.
5. Sprinkle with lemon zest for a burst of fresh flavor.

This rice dish may not be the most exciting, but it's a surefire way to add some green to your soul!

Chapter 8

Ten, Nine, Eight . . . **Hypnosis!**

And here we go again: I hear a friend has lost weight, I want to do the same, so I ask for advice, she recommends something, I try it, and nothing. The cycle repeats. But this time my friend was enthusing about a hypnotist she'd seen, claiming the visit life-changing, with her chakras and emotional blockages miraculously having opened up. And guess what? It worked . . . for her. She spoke at length about hypnosis and the subconscious in a slow, dreamy manner, suggesting that my inability to lose weight may be rooted in my lack of understanding of the underlying issue. Joining support groups, posting on forums, or starving myself won't make a difference, she said. Maybe, she claimed, centuries ago, I was a starving child and now, subconsciously, I sabotage every diet I try so I won't have to relive that hunger. Or perhaps, in a past life, I was a noblewoman from the Loire Valley in France who relished fine cuisine and my soul yearns to return there. I had to admit, she might be on to something, especially with the noblewoman hypothesis. It was worth a shot.

I quickly dialed the hypnotist's number, eager for an appointment that couldn't wait. Despite my pleas and reasons, the sought-after hypnotist was fully booked. Apparently, I wasn't the only one in the area dealing with this issue. In the meantime, I abandoned any thoughts of dieting. What was the point? My subconscious was clearly at the helm. I indulged in all the delicious foods I'd been depriving myself of, perhaps for centuries. By the time my appointment finally came, I'd put on a few extra pounds and was ready to see what the hypnotist could do for me.

Feeling nervous, I sat in the waiting room, which was shared with other professionals, like accountants and ophthalmologists. I tried my best to conceal the true reason for my visit from the receptionists. Was I the only one there for the hypnotist? Finally, he entered the waiting room, and I was pleasantly surprised. He was a well-dressed and well-groomed man in his 40s, far from the eccentric hypnotists I remembered from my childhood who would mesmerize their volunteers on stage with their intense gaze and soothing voice. This man exuded an air of normalcy and groundedness.

I followed him eagerly, like a kid promised a treat.

How did I fall for this again? How do I keep believing, hoping, expecting anew each time? Well, I'll spare you the details, as there's simply nothing to tell. After being informed that my problem was too complicated to solve in a single session, I reluctantly handed over a considerable sum for five more sessions. Despite my best efforts, I couldn't reach a hypnotic state where I wasn't fully conscious, nor could I comprehend his instructions to stop eating when I felt 80 percent full. He wasn't even able to uncover intriguing stories from my past lives. No, I was stuck with the same old childhood issues that I openly share with anyone who listens on a daily basis.

My cognitive dissonance was in overdrive, and I couldn't bring myself to admit to my friends and family, who were all waiting in anticipation for tales of my hypnotic journey, that the experience was profoundly uneventful. So, I attempted to downplay it, insisting it was "effective" and "real"—anything to divert their attention (and mine) from the fact that I failed again. I said goodbye to dining at fancy restaurants, not just because I was in control but mainly because I couldn't afford them anymore. I stopped eating at 80% full, but it wasn't subconscious. I did it very much on purpose because I was too embarrassed my family and friends would know I'd fallen for another trick.

Now, as I share with my students the wisdom of the Blue Zones—the regions of the world where people live the longest, healthiest lives—I always underscore the Okinawan phrase for *bon appetit:* Hara Hachi Bu, which translates to "Eat until you're 80 percent full." Those Okinawans are onto something, or perhaps hypnosis just works better for them. Regardless, my students received this advice for far less than I paid for it.

But I couldn't resist for long. You might find it hard to believe, and perhaps now is a good time to set this book aside because the author is clearly not all there, but here's a secret: after that experience, I tried hypnosis two more times. Yes, I'm serious.

Drum roll! Allow me to introduce you to "the Mad Russian" from Boston. He was reputed to be a wizard who could free people from addictions to smoking, alcohol, sugar, carbohydrates, and assist with weight loss and other addictions. So, naturally, I had to go. More precisely, I flew. I boarded a plane for this. However, I must credit him for the unbelievably low fee he charged $80, with the potential for free reinforcement and support for life. I thought, this must be a sign that he truly knows his stuff; otherwise, he would have been out of business a long time ago.

When I arrived, I was amazed to find a packed

waiting room with about 30 people, each seeking a different kind of rehabilitation. The Mad Russian came out, gave a brief talk, and explained his method. He asked us to decide in advance what addiction we wanted to eliminate for good—this was crucial. We had to commit to eradicating our addiction permanently. But, as a Libra, I struggled with making that decision or uttering the words "always" or "forever." Yes, I wanted to quit drinking, but what was the point if I couldn't have a little wine during dry periods, maybe just a small glass daily? I didn't want carbs at the moment, but I wanted to enjoy pasta when I visited Italy without breaking the spell. Couldn't I just indulge a little? Be half-pregnant?

We entered the maestro's room one by one, hoping to be liberated from our vices. When my turn came, I found myself standing in front of him, a charismatic and handsome man in his 70's, feeling unexpectedly shy and wondering what had brought me to this room. "Yes, young lady," he began. "How can I assist you?"

"I want to lose 15 pounds," I said quietly. I stumbled over my words, trying to express my desire to lose weight but also wanting to keep my wine. "Can I still have a glass, or maybe two?" I stammered.

The Russian looked at me with a twinkle in his eyes and said, "Why do you want to lose weight? You are a beautiful woman." This caught me off guard and made me question his intentions. But he continued, "Do men really appreciate thin women? When you see a thin and perfect woman walk into a room, do you actually like her?"

"Not really," I admitted, feeling a bit foolish.

"So is that truly what you desire?" he asked, his voice gentle but firm.

I hadn't considered it from that perspective before, and if I'm being honest, he had a point. However, since I had already made the journey to Boston, I figured I might as well make the most of it. I asked him to work his magic. He told me to close my eyes, think about what I wanted to let go of and what I wanted to keep, and then, with a snap of his fingers, he said, "Go home, but remember what I told you."

Naturally, it didn't work—I wasn't ready to give up anything at that time. But that encounter with the Mad Russian was a turning point for me, a lesson that has stayed with me ever since. And for only $80, I'd say it was a pretty good deal.

Perfectly Imperfect

In that room, with the Mad Russian, I came to understand that perhaps it was I who was the mad one between us. What lengths was I willing to go to shed weight, and why was he advising me against it? Even though his income hinged on customers like me, he was speaking the truth. It resonated with me and allowed me to see myself through a different lens.

Do we truly prefer perfection over imperfection? Do we only connect with those who appear flawless? The truth is, imperfections—a wrinkle, a crooked tooth, slightly close-set eyes—these are what make us human, and that's real life. The Japanese recognized this centuries ago when they introduced the concept of "Wabi Sabi." There are different interpretations of the notion, some suggesting the golden repairs that bring grace and elegance to a broken vase. But it goes deeper than that. The Japanese embrace transience and imperfection as qualities that evoke beauty and intrigue; a longing that arises when we encounter something slightly flawed, slightly rugged, authentic, and ephemeral. It's an acceptance of aging. In her book *Wabi Sabi: Japanese Wisdom for a Perfectly Imperfect Life,* Beth Kempton explores the principles of the Japanese way of life and how we can incorporate them into our own existence (6). This philosophy encourages us to observe the world and appreciate the beauty in simplicity, nature, and existence itself. It shows us how to cherish perfect moments in an imperfect world, appreciating the beauty in places, objects, and people.

Since embracing this outlook, I have felt a profound sense of tranquility. I now perceive people, places, and even myself in a completely different way. I have let go of excess belongings and chosen a more comfortable lifestyle that allows me to find beauty in the simple things. Instead of trying to hide every wrinkle and flaw, I have come to embrace them with fondness, recognizing the beauty in aging. I strive to see the beauty in its entirety and celebrate it.

For Reflection and Self-Work

1. How comfortable are you with embracing your imperfections?

2. How do you handle perceived flaws or imperfections in yourself and others?

3. Can you identify any quirks or imperfections that you personally find endearing?

For Reflection and Self-Work

4. Do you see the beauty in small imperfections or quirks in others?

5. Would you like to see more of these imperfections embraced in society and in yourself?

Recipe

Negroni Cocktail Recipe
Mesmerize and Hypnotize Your Guests

Ingredients:

- 1 oz Campari
- 1 oz gin
- 1 oz red vermouth
- Ice
- 1 large square ice cube, for serving
- Orange peel twist

Instructions:

1. In a mixing glass, combine Campari, gin, and red vermouth.
2. Stir the mixture with a bar spoon over ice until well chilled.
3. Place a large square ice cube in an old-fashioned glass.
4. Strain the chilled cocktail mixture into the glass with the large ice cube.
5. Garnish with an orange peel twist.
6. Serve and enjoy!

Chapter 9

Visits to Israel, or "Tami, You've Filled Out a Bit!"

For the past three decades, I have made my home in Miami with my family, but every year, I eagerly embark on a journey back to my homeland—Israel. In preparation, I start with a new plan to shed a few pounds before I encounter the looks and comments that greet me upon arrival. I'm all too familiar with the scrutinizing gazes, the elevator looks, and the customary comments: "You've lost weight!" "You've filled out a bit, haven't you?" Why? Why can't someone simply say "You look great," "You're glowing," or "You look happy"? Why must there always be comments about my weight and unsolicited opinions? The same goes for remarks about weight loss; it's as if I was fat the last time you saw me. Thanks for the compliment, but no thanks. Nevertheless, my pre-travel weight-loss rituals used to look like this:

Two months before: I would embark on a crash diet and start a strict walking routine with unusual determination. Excuses were not an option, and I refused to deviate from my plan. I needed results and fast! With the upcoming date of my trip engraved in my mind, just the thought of incurring hundreds of dollars in change fees strengthened my resolve.

Day of the flight: I slip into some slimming black leggings, trying to strike the balance between comfort and not looking like I just rolled out of bed. In my luggage, I pack a pair of stylish jeans and sleek heeled boots (it's not that I weigh a lot relative to my height; I'm just short for my weight—heels are a good solution). Armed with bags of sliced veggies, nuts, and rice cakes, I set off on my journey.

On the flight: I stick to just water, avoiding the wine and meal offered. Low-carb, low-fat, low-salt is my mantra these days. How do I pass the time during this long flight? The only thing that works for me is a sleeping pill, and soon enough, I fall into a deep slumber until I finally land in Tel Aviv—hungry but happy.

We've made it! My schedule is jam-packed with meetings in the first couple of days. I've got to see my family and closest friends before I dip some pita bread in the delicious hummus. My trusty jeans hold up for just three days before the feasting begins: famous Israeli breakfasts, endless gatherings at the local café for some fresh coffee and pastries, Mediterranean street food, and fresh bread at the farmers' market. Oh, and of course, extravagant late-night dinners with plenty of alcohol and wonderful dishes from the creative Israeli cuisine. Despite the financial toll, puffy eyes, added weight, and a cough from the cigarette smoke (yes, people still do that here), I enjoy every moment. I tuck away my jeans at the bottom of my suitcase, break out the comfy leggings and oversized T-shirt, and arm myself with a bottle of Pepto Bismol to endure the inevitable stomachaches. Life is just too good to resist.

"Vow-breaking trips"—that's what I call my visits to Israel because of all the promises and vows I make before the trip to avoid the tempting dishes, to stay active, and to drink only one glass of wine a night. They all go out the window the moment I touch down in the delectable Israeli heaven.

☛ When Your Friends Turn into Workout Fanatics

Over the years, the divide among my Israeli friends has grown wider. On one side, you have the fitness enthusiasts: runners, cyclists, Iron Man competitors, you name it. Every time we meet, they boast about their latest athletic achievements—the kilometers they've clocked, the weight they've lifted, the thrill of running up those scorching steps in summer. And of course, there's always a grueling workout session to cap it off, followed by trips to the New York Marathon or the Tour de France. Meanwhile, I find comfort in the fact that there are also friends who are more like me—those who've grown a little plumper, grown tired of trying to impress, embraced self-love, and stopped obsessing over their six-pack. I'm not saying you should give up on exercise and healthy eating. I just don't subscribe to the obsession. So, I walk the streets, I breathe in the scents of spring and autumn, I savor the sights and sounds of the city, the markets, the port. I recall my childhood memories, the songs, the good old days, and a tinge of sadness and longing creeps into my heart. So I comfort myself with my favorite street food, a nod to my childhood, or a seaside popsicle—a reminder of my father on beach vacations, of beautiful days that have passed by so quickly.

☛ Swing by Tonight?

At every meal, my hosts spare no effort in delighting me. But if I dare to suggest that I'm practicing a bit of restraint, or, God forbid, have cut back on alcohol this week, or perhaps even made the audacious resolution to abstain from dining after 11:30 at night, I'm met with cries of "What's gotten into you?" or "You're no fun anymore!" or "You're turning into a real American—dinner at five!"

So, what's a people-pleaser like me supposed to do? I offer to bring some salad or other healthy options, make excuses, but in the end, I always fall prey to temptation and surrender to the feast laid before me. I keep trying to be good, knowing I will eventually cave in.

Here are some witty excuses I've adopted for when I really don't want to say, "I'm on a diet":

- "No alcohol; I'm on antibiotics."
- "I'm allergic to sugar/cheese/strawberries/chocolate."
- "I just had a huge late lunch."
- "I have a colonoscopy tomorrow!"

On the return flight to the US, I'm dressed in my comfortable drawstrings and my husband's cozy sweatshirt, wasting no time kicking things off with a drink and some nuts as soon as we take off. I enjoy the entire meal and wash it down with a glass or two of wine and the tube of Swiss chocolate I picked up at duty-free. By the end of my 13-hour flight, I'm exhausted and ready to go out for some good old

American grub maybe a burger or BBQ ribs before I start my diet . . . tomorrow.

What's Five Pounds When You've Got Family?

It's not that I lack conviction. I know how to say "no" when I really want to, but the question is, do I really want to? Do I choose to avoid the risk of gaining a few extra pounds over cherishing moments with the people I love? Is going down a size worth the cost of missing out on time with those closest to me?

I'm lucky. Truly lucky. I have been blessed with people around me whom I love and who love me. Relationships are complex and require effort—whether it's between friends, spouses, neighbors, or partners. We all need them. As the English poet John Donne wrote in the 17th century, "No man is an island"(7)—we are all interconnected, and each individual is a part of the world and the whole.

A landmark study conducted at Harvard University starting in 1938 tested over 700 participants over the course of 80 years to understand the factors affecting their health, careers, marriages, and other aspects of their lives (8). The results were surprising and showed the importance of positive and happy relationships over other factors such as money, fame, social status,

IQ, and even genetics. The researchers concluded that close relationships—more than any other factor—are the top predictor of good health, happiness, and longevity.

Every year, the Global Happiness Index sheds light on over 200 countries, ranking them based on various criteria. As an Israeli, I was surprised to see my country consistently ranked proudly among the top 15 countries in the world. Is it because of the wealth of the national economy? No. Is it because there is no existential danger or threat? Of course not. Is life expectancy there above average? Nope. The real secret to Israel's happiness lies in the strong bonds of family and friendship woven into the fabric of their society. From the joyous Shabbat dinners shared with loved ones to the simple act of asking a neighbor for a cup of sugar or to look after a child, it's these connections that bring true happiness. Even among the Israeli diaspora, including myself, the close-knit bonds we carry with us from our homeland remain steadfast. Relationships take effort, from showing up when called upon to making the investment of time and care, even if it means gaining a few extra pounds along the way.

For Reflection and Self-Work

1. Are you making a deliberate enough effort to strengthen the bonds with those dear to you?

2. How frequently do you spend quality time with friends and family members?

3. When was the most recent occasion where you planned a joyful family or social gathering?

4. What is your preferred activity during these gatherings? (Singing, cooking, dining, talking, or watching movies?)

____

____

It's time to mark the next reunion in your calendar. Don't take your friendships for granted invest in them.

Recipe

My Famous Party **Pleaser Salad**

Ingredients:

· Baby mixed greens

· 1 carrot, grated

· Crumbled goat's cheese

· 1/2 cup honey roasted peanuts or candied pecans

Dressing Ingredients:

(Depending on the number of people and size of the salad, I like to make the dressing at this quantity. Drizzle and toss the necessary amount with the salad and keep the rest in the fridge)

· 1/3 cup balsamic vinegar

· 1 crushed garlic clove

· 2/3 cup olive oil

· 1 teaspoon honey or maple syrup

Recipe

My Famous Party **Pleaser Salad**

Instructions:

1. In a large bowl, mix the baby leaves and grated carrot.
2. In a jar with a lid, shake all the dressing ingredients together.
3. Right before serving, pour the dressing on the salad and top with the crumbled goat cheese and nuts.
4. Enjoy the salad as a filling alternative to the tempting call of bread and pastries.

Chapter 10

Chew 30 Times,or the **Mindfulness Diet**

Some years ago, my friend (the perpetually slim one, mind—you what did she know of the struggle?) and I stumbled upon a health magazine that extolled the virtues of chewing each bite of food 30 times. It promised health and, oh-so-alluringly, a slimmer figure. For someone like me, who tends to do everything quickly—talking, writing, working, cooking, and eating—this concept seemed foreign. Taking my time? Not my style. It's not as if this fast-paced lifestyle was only during my years of raising children and juggling multiple tasks. No, I've always been this way. In fact, I consider it an achievement if I chew a bite of food five times, so the idea of 30 chews seemed quite ambitious. Nevertheless, my friend and I agreed to give it a try for two weeks, with a twist: we would only eat what our bodies truly craved. This meant being mindful of whether we were eating out of genuine hunger or for other reasons, such as enticing flavors, feeling obligated to finish our plates, mistaking fullness for emptiness, or even eating due to emotions like nerves or joy. It was a brilliant idea, but the implementation proved to be a bit clumsy. Here's how it worked:

Each bite was laboriously chewed 30 times, reducing it to an unrecognizable liquid. Voilà, a steak smoothie! But wait, there's more. Between each bite, we probed our souls, asking: are we genuinely still hungry? If the answer was "yes," we forged ahead to the next bite and repeated the 30-chew ritual. If, however, we admitted that we weren't quite hungry anymore, we pushed our plates aside and abandoned the meal. The leftovers could be given to the dog, saved for later, shared with neighbors, or, regrettable, thrown away.

☛ How Can I Throw Away Food?

Yes, throwing away food can be a difficult thing to accept. "Don't waste food" is a mantra that many of us were raised with, along with "clean your plate." We've all heard it, regardless of our background or upbringing, whether it came from war veterans or Holocaust survivors. This sentiment was deeply ingrained in me as I grew up in Israel, a country familiar with scarcity and people who experienced hunger firsthand. It took me years to understand that overeating and stuffing myself until I was uncomfortably full would only result in weight gain. That's it. No one benefits from it, and it certainly doesn't feed a famished child in the world.

If no one wanted the leftovers and they weren't going to be eaten soon, I would transfer them to a smaller container and put them in the freezer. But inevitably, they would go untouched, and I would end up having to throw them away and wash yet another container.

So, I resolved not to become a receptacle for leftovers, and that's how I raised my kids: start with a small portion; don't let your eyes deceive you. And when you're not hungry anymore, don't force yourself to finish. Yes, my children are slim, but perhaps that's also because 50 percent of their genes didn't come from me.

This painstaking routine persisted for a month. It was far from easy, but the results were astounding. I shed some pounds and felt fantastic. I discovered a remarkable sense of lightness, realizing I was nourishing my body with only what it needed, which turned out to be surprisingly little. I'm not sure if the frenzied chewing was actually the magic bullet, but I'm confident that being mindful of my intake and listening to my body's signals made all the difference.

This lifestyle isn't entirely sustainable, though, and I quickly reverted to my old habits, eating quickly and impulsively. Remember the hypnotist who tried to teach my brain to detect when I was 80 percent full? Fundamentally, it's the same idea, but approached in very different ways. The first focuses on self-awareness and conscious thought while the latter bypasses thought altogether, entrusting the task to the subconscious (which, in my case, seemed to have taken an extended vacation). Now, after many years and countless studies validating the effects of mindfulness, I realize we were on the brink of something life-changing.

Single is the New Multi

Have you noticed? Life moves fast. We're trained to multitask, but what does that really mean? Managing multiple tasks simultaneously, but not succeeding in any. When I'm not paying attention, I find myself trying to multitask like a juggler. Driving with one hand on the steering wheel, applying makeup with the other, tossing pretzels to the kids in the back, eavesdropping on their conversations, or flipping through radio stations. Far from ideal. It's even worse when we're having a conversation with a friend, half-heartedly watching a forwarded video, listening to our child's stories from school, or attempting a crossword puzzle during dinner with our spouse. The solution?

Mindfulness. It has become a buzzword, the hot topic of the day. Everyone is talking about it, writing about it, and practicing it. But what does it really mean?

Mindfulness is the ability to live in the present moment without judging it. To simply exist, without categorizing the experience as good or bad, or trying to change it. Of course, we can achieve mindfulness through meditation, but I struggle to commit to that type of practice. My attempts to sit still for 20 minutes often turn into scratching my back or mentally updating my shopping list. My preferred path to mindfulness? Single-tasking. When I read a book, I drown out external noise and immerse myself in the pages. When I'm writing, I switch my phone to airplane mode so that I don't need to resist reacting to every pinging notification. I am fully present.

As for food, mindful eating is one of the healthiest and most rewarding approaches. Most of us eat on autopilot. Who among us hasn't raided the fridge for a snack while listening to a friend's heartfelt troubles on the phone? Or, in moments of stress, finish an entire box of cashews reserved for that evening's guests?

It's not just what we eat that matters, but why and how. Complete awareness and zero distractions are key. This applies not only during meals with family and friends but especially when dining alone. When was the last time you sat with yourself at a table with nice tableware—without a phone, TV, or even a book? (In the past, it was the newspaper). When did you last focus solely on your meal, savoring it, appreciating its texture, flavor, and nourishment, rather than mindlessly consuming it while scrolling Facebook?

In the Blue Zone challenges I lead, I encourage participants to enjoy two screen-free meals during the first week. Just two! Sounds difficult? Many report it's the hardest part of the challenge. Naturally, kids mirror this behavior, glued to their phones during family dinners.

I'm always taken aback when I see a mother and daughter, a young couple on a date, or friends taking a true lunch break to enjoy some quality time, all sitting in a restaurant, each engrossed in their phones. We need to adopt savoring not only for our meals but also for other aspects of life. I strive to apply this concept to my relationships, time, and experiences. I savor them. I appreciate the taste and aroma of the moment. I savor my vacation by fully enjoying trips without constantly snapping photos for Facebook. I try to engage in uninterrupted conversations with dear friends. I make an effort to stay present, though it's not always easy or instinctive. I often find myself sneakily liking a friend's post during a Zoom lecture or scrolling through stories, sometimes even messaging multiple people simultaneously. Or, while on a dream vacation, instead of appreciating the view from my expensive hotel window, I'm browsing Hotels.com for my next getaway.

Ever heard of FOMO (Fear of Missing Out)? That nagging feeling that, while enjoying dinner at a restaurant, there might be a superior one nearby? Or that, while hanging out with friends, you could be attending a lively party? FOMO keeps us restless, perpetually seeking the next best thing. Let's embrace JOMO (Joy of Missing Out) instead: the delight in being present, without chasing after every experience. I recommend savoring the little things, appreciating what is rather than what could have been.

For Reflection and Self-Work

1. What multitasking activities do you engage in throughout the day?

2. Are all of them truly necessary?

3. Which tasks can you shift from multitasking to single-tasking in your life?

For Reflection and Self-Work

4. How would you feel on a trip without your phone or taking selfies? Enjoying your morning coffee without a phone or newspaper? Eating a meal at the table with silverware and a napkin, rather than standing or in the car? Can you think of other examples?

The Chew-30-Times Diet:
Why try: Enhances mindfulness, aids digestion, promotes overall health, and supports weight loss.
Why not: Tiresome, awkward in social settings, and mildly obsessive.

Recipe

Healthy Quinoa Salad That Needs to Be Chewed

Ingredients for Quinoa:

- 1 cup quinoa (white or colored)
- 2 cups of water
- 1 teaspoon of salt
- 1 tablespoon olive oil

Quinoa Preparation:

1. In a pot, heat the olive oil and lightly toast the quinoa.
2. Add water and salt, then bring to a boil.
3. Reduce the heat, cover the pot, and cook for 20 minutes (similar to cooking rice).
4. Let the quinoa cool.

Ingredients for the Salad:

- 1/2 cup cooked chickpeas
- 1 small tart green apple
- 2 stalks of celery
- 1 carrot
- 1 red onion
- A bunch of mint

Recipe

Healthy Quinoa Salad That Needs to Be Chewed

- A bunch of cilantro
- 1/2 cup cranberries or goji berries
- 1/2 cup roasted hazelnuts

Ingredients for the Dressing:

- 1 teaspoon of freshly grated ginger
- 1 tablespoon organic natural maple syrup
- 1 clove of garlic
- Juice of 2 lemons or limes
- 1/2 cup of fine olive oil

Salad Preparation:

1. Mix all the salad ingredients with the cooled quinoa.
2. Combine and whisk together the dressing ingredients.
3. Pour the dressing over the salad and mix well.
4. Serve and remember to chew 30 times!

Chapter 11

Pills, Shots, and Injections, Oh My!

I'm not particularly proud of this next anecdote, but in my defense, any pills and injections I've taken have always been under the careful watch of a medical professional (cardiologists or endocrinologists—I never compromise on my health).

The process is always the same. I undergo comprehensive lab tests, secretly hoping the doctor will uncover an inherent issue with my metabolism or identify a critical element that is vital for weight loss. For better or worse, my healthy body reveals no such problems. "Tamar," the doctor informs me, "the issue lies in your mind, not your body. You enjoy life too much, and you need to rein it in." Then, he prescribes pills to boost my metabolism and suppress my appetite. But do these pills really have to destroy my love for life? I am not eager to go down this road, especially not for the second or third time when I've already discovered that it only works for about a month. But, just like how

I forgot the pain of my eldest son's birth and returned a year later for another, my memory operates in mysterious ways, failing to recall my previous misadventures in the realm of diets.

At this point, the doctor prescribes a low-calorie diet devoid of carbohydrates, fats, and any real flavor, bills my credit card (which conveniently has no memory either) for three months in advance and gives me pills for every possible ailment and condition under the sun.

I'm genuinely excited; this time will be different, I'm sure of it. But it's not. The pills make me jittery, dry my mouth, and reduce my patience to that of a ballistic missile. On the upside, I genuinely have no appetite. But there's also no joy in life, no nourishment, no pleasure, nothing! Then, the worry sets in. Is this really healthy at all? How do I get my vitamins from a meager 800 calories a day? Could it be addictive? And what if I go off the rails? (Would anyone even notice?) In short, it's a mess.

I lose weight steadily in the first month, but then I hit a plateau and start blaming myself for consuming 817 calories the previous day instead of the prescribed 800. I convince myself that this is why nothing is working. Well, if I have already crossed the line, I might as well jump in with both feet. And the truth is it's really,

really unfair! I follow all the instructions, but this little voice in my head convinces me that it's my fault, that I was not completely devoted and committed to the plan. And overall, what kind of mother am I? Risking my health for some foolish vanity, squandering the inheritance, and not even seeing any results. "So," the voice tells me, "just give up already. It's not worth it. Treat yourself a little. It's not working anyway." And this is where I encounter the ultimate obstacle that sabotages every diet, every time, without fail. The most dangerous sentence we can tell ourselves: "What the hell, I might as well." And off I go.

Sound familiar? In that moment, it truly is delightful. But then, the dam bursts, and weeks of deprivation and abstinence disappear in an instant. It starts with something salty, moves to something sweet, jumps to something sour, a bit sweeter, and then finally, a glass of whiskey. My stomach feels satisfied, and I feel relaxed, falling asleep as content as a baby after a warm bottle of milk. If it ended here, there wouldn't be much of a problem, but it doesn't. When the dam breaks, that small hole just gets bigger, and I am liberated.

☛ From Pills to Shots, the Journey Is Indeed a Short One

Don't worry, I'm not the only nutcase here. The world went wild over the HCG hormone diet.
What, you didn't try that too? Where have you been? It started quietly, under the radar, and eventually became mainstream. All my friends either injected the hormone or took it as drops under their tongues. We're not exactly the epitome of sanity; we've already established that. Dealing with the injections was one thing, but sticking to a mere 500-calorie-a-day diet felt a little extreme. I received a bag filled with syringes, hormone vials worth their weight in gold, and a page with diet instructions. Just to reiterate: it was a 500-calorie-a-day diet.

I lost weight during the first two weeks, quite a lot actually, but then, as always, my body adjusted and decided that even 500 calories were too much, refusing to shed any more weight. I hit a plateau. But there was a solution for that too: apple day. My poor body, I sincerely apologize for all the torment I put you through, but for apple day, I apologize twice as much. Apples are hard to digest and rich in fiber, which always gave me stomachaches. One apple would make me uncomfortable, so five? But it was prescribed in all of the plateau literature. No questions asked.

I remember going to work with four green apples, hoping that the plateau would quickly subside. By four o'clock, I was
on the floor, not from laughter but from stomach pain. I couldn't move. I crawled into the car and somehow managed to make it home. Barely able to find the Fernet Branca, that aromatic and bitter herbal liqueur from Italy, which always worked like magic for me, instantly relieving stomach cramps. I took a small shot —it didn't help. One more, another half-cup—voila! The stomach pain faded away, and I, tipsy from the 40% alcohol, fell asleep until the next day.

Perhaps some wise spirit or grandmotherly figure visited me in a dream because I woke up with a clear mind. I tossed the syringes and vials, shredded the instruction sheet into tiny pieces, made myself a cup of coffee with milk and toast (which the previous day would have exceeded my daily calorie intake), and swore off this particular madness. And I held firm. I found other fads, but I never returned to pills or dangerous starvation methods. Any diet or nutritional approach should be enjoyable. We can't endure pain solely to attain a goal. Life is too short, and we deserve to enjoy the journey.

☛ We're All Moving Targets

We all have goals and aspirations that we work towards. We are taught to set goals, document them, break them down into manageable steps, and systematically check them off our lists. But are these goals truly what we want? Are they driven by the expectations of others or societal norms? Are they aligned with our values and authentic selves?

It is important to ask ourselves these questions and set goals that come from within us and resonate with our true selves.

This, however, gives rise to other questions. Do the ends truly justify the means? Are we solely focused on achieving the goal? And what happens after we reach it? Often, we find ourselves striving for a new goal, whether it's losing a few more pounds or getting rid of a few more wrinkles. This applies not just to dieting, but to all aspects of life.

The truth is it's never enough, and the goalposts are always moving. We can choose to keep chasing after them, or perhaps we won't. The key is to savor the journey. Sometimes, the path itself is so rewarding that we don't feel the need to rush towards the destination. And when the road is filled with challenges and obstacles that cause more suffering than pleasure, we become laser-focused on the goal and grit our teeth through the hardships until we reach it.

Remember the Journey

It's important to remember that happiness is not about reaching the peak; it's about enjoying the climb towards a destination that truly matters to us. As Dr. Tal Ben-Shahar says, "Happiness is the experience of climbing towards the destination." (9) The journey itself is the goal, but that doesn't mean we should disregard the importance of the destination. It guides us and helps us achieve results. In the context of dieting, even if we have set a goal that is genuinely important to us, like losing 15 pounds, we should not subject ourselves to unnecessary suffering. We should believe that there is a more enjoyable way to achieve weight loss, even if it takes longer.

It took me many years to recognize how I mistreated and disrespected my body, debasing myself by injecting and starving it while shamelessly manipulating it. However, since then, I've matured and gained wisdom. I've grown tired of the shortcut route and am now set on the high road.

For Reflection and Self-Work

1. When does that little voice in your head appear, and what does it say?

2. How do you interact with that voice? Do you listen, argue, or accept it as a part of yourself?

3. Share an example of a goal you've achieved in your life. Did you enjoy the journey? To what extent?

4. Do you also see the journey as an end in itself? How can you make it more enjoyable?

Pills, Shots, and Starvation:
Why try? No reason.
Why not? All the reasons in the world.

Recipe

Healthy Ice Cream That Sweetens My Journey

- Small bag of frozen berries (strawberries, blueberries, raspberries, or your choice)
- 2 Medjool dates, pitted
- 1/2 cup coconut milk

Ingredients:

1. Place all the ingredients in a powerful blender.
2. Blend for a few minutes at high speed (you can use a tamper or add a little more coconut milk as needed). Aim for a slightly textured consistency where you can still feel the pieces of fruit and dates.
3. Serve in a beautiful martini glass and sprinkle unsweetened ground coconut on top.
   If this isn't a pleasant journey, I don't know what is!

Chapter 12

I Thought I Was Just a **Basic Girl**

During lunch about a decade ago, I saw my brother (yes, the slim one) enjoying unusual foods like a sprouted tortilla with avocado, instead of the usual greasy, meat-filled sandwich. Intrigued by his sudden change, I asked him why. He told me that he had recently come across a life-changing book given to him by a friend. He had embraced a new nutritional philosophy and was feeling amazing. To my surprise (and slight annoyance), he had already lost five pounds.

Predictably, as had happened many times before, I found myself deep in another book, buying into another approach, more research, and more allegedly groundbreaking scientific revelations. This time, the revolution centered around alkalinity versus acidity.

The author of the book, was subsequently convicted for practicing medicine without a license and without the doctoral degree he claimed (which, I must admit, initially impressed me). His teachings weren't part of any reputable university curriculum, but at that point, I was still intrigued and readily consumed his theory. He proposed that the root of all diseases and obesity was the acidity in our bodies, causing havoc, illnesses, and inflammation. Apparently, bacteria flourish in an acidic environment. The theory posited that acidity-inducing foods were, naturally, all the delectable ones—sugar, meat, eggs, white flour, simple carbohydrates, dairy products, and inevitably, alcohol in every form. Conversely, foods promoting alkalinity were primarily green vegetables, almonds, grapefruit, tomatoes, lemon (surprisingly, right?), coconut, sprouted seeds, and so on.

The theory also argued that it wasn't just food, but also our thoughts, social circles, exercise (which is crucial), as well as relaxation and meditation, that influenced our acidity and alkalinity levels. Now, I'm not a scientist, so I can't confirm or refute the scientific accuracy of this theory. However, I do know that I was completely captivated by this fascinating concept. Everyone knows how to pinpoint a problem and reel me in. "Have you tried every possible diet and failed to lose weight?" Absolutely! "Do you struggle to lose weight even when following a strict calorie intake? Do you sometimes even gain weight despite being incredibly disciplined?" Stop right there. That's exactly it! How does he know?

After spending half of the book identifying the problem, the authors typically offer a solution that they have considered for anywhere from an hour to a few years. The presentation of these solutions seems so straightforward and logical, and as a result, I wholeheartedly embrace the ideas and passionately advocate for them to anyone who will listen. I have become skilled in the art of cognitive dissonance. This book not only promised a diet, but also guaranteed miracles. Being a firm believer in miracles and someone who never does anything without 100 percent commitment (if you hadn't already noticed), I plunged in wholeheartedly.

California, Here We Come

I soon discovered that this esteemed doctor organized workshops and retreats at his farm in California. Despite his prominent status, you could actually visit his property and participate (while surrendering several thousand acidic dollars). It seemed perfectly reasonable for me to register and dive straight in! A good friend of mine, who suffers from diabetes and follows all my shenanigans, was quickly persuaded to join me. And so, we boarded a flight destined for

California. Come on, what's a six-hour flight, a hotel room, and leaving the kids at home compared to the promise of health and slimness, especially if you're hopelessly acidic?

Upon arrival at the farmhouse home, where the doctor's wife served as the resident cook, I recognized within the first hour that perhaps I wasn't quite in the right place. Surrounded by people grappling with serious conditions like diabetes and cancer, seeking healing through dietary changes, I found myself there to—it's somewhat embarrassing to admit—lose 10 pounds? Is there no end to my naivety? It felt wrong to share my true motivations to the group, especially considering the grave health concerns of others. What could I possibly say? Instead, I tweaked my narrative slightly: "I'm here to take preventive steps towards a healthier life." That sounded considerably better than "I'm here to fit into size six jeans." But to you, I promise nothing but the truth, the whole truth, without any embellishment. Just how far am I willing to go?

Over the next four days, we consumed endless amounts of water mixed with green powder, tinged with spirulina algae, French clay from some mountain, and a hint of lemon for flavor. Our meals consisted of buckwheat and lettuce (I despise buckwheat). We jumped on a trampoline, enjoyed saunas and lymphatic massages, and had grapefruit for dessert. I managed to lose five pounds and went completely off the deep end. I brought home a trampoline, a luxurious infrared sauna (anyone interested? It's a bit too hot for Miami), a professional water filter, spirulina powder, clay powder (I've got lemons too), a sprouting device, a dehydrator, a slow cooker—in other words, I've secured the doctor's financial future. My friend's sugar levels improved, and she decided to buy some supplements, too. So, light-hearted and content, we returned home. All humor aside, I firmly believe that a balanced diet, positive thoughts, walks in nature, and good company contribute to longevity. However, that lesson was one of the costliest, and the feeling of being swindled didn't really help me feel good either.

White Coat Syndrome

What is it about the white coat that captures our attention so? Is it the assumed authority that lures us in? Are we more predisposed to trust someone we perceive as an authority rather than just an average Joe?

The Milgram experiment, conducted by psychologist Stanley Milgram of Yale University, probed the extent to which participants would obey those deemed authoritative, the degree of harm they could inflict on others, and the limits of their compliance (10). Without going into the comprehensive details, participants, oblivious they were part of an experiment, were told to administer a supposedly harmless mild electric shock to "students" (actually actors) whenever they failed to complete a given task. A man in a white coat, whom the participants believed to be a doctor, reassured them that everything was safe and they had nothing to fret over. He ordered them to progressively increase the intensity of the shock, and the "students" reacted with escalating severity. The ghastly outcome: 65 percent of the participants complied and cranked up the shock strength until the "student" was motionless on the floor, and they were instructed to stop.

Milgram's study raised a number of ethical questions and shook the very foundation of the research community. My takeaway? I'm not the only one. Many of us probably harbor an inherent tendency to trust authority figures, which can be potentially dangerous. Fortunately, my losses were confined to money and a bit of time, and I escaped unscathed (I still use the alkaline filter).

Nonetheless, this experience taught me to keep my eyes wide open, use my critical thinking skills, and verify everything twice. I learned not to take things at face value and to avoid making assumptions, particularly when it involves my health and my body, which has already suffered the consequences of being gullible at times. A piece of advice: it's wise to learn from others' experiences. You don't personally need to try everything. For instance, you really shouldn't drink French clay. Let me state that for the records. It's disgusting.

For Reflection and Self-Work

1. Ask yourself honestly: How do you deal with authority? Do you comply anyway?

2. Whom do you consider authoritative figures?

3. How do you validate and confirm authority?

4. Are there any people or relationships in your life that are toxic or negative that need to be addressed or ended?

Recipe

Buckwheat Bowl
Yes, Buckwheat.

Ingredients:

- 1 cup buckwheat groats
- 1 and 3/4 cups water
- 1/2 ripe avocado, diced
- 10 cherry tomatoes, halved
- 2 tablespoons cold-pressed organic olive oil
- Pinch of sea salt
- 2 tablespoons slivered almonds

Instructions:

1. Rinse the buckwheat groats and place them in a saucepan with 1 and 3/4 cups of water. Bring to a boil, then reduce heat to low and simmer for 10–15 minutes, or until the water has been absorbed, and the buckwheat is tender.
2. In a bowl, combine the cooked buckwheat, diced avocado, and halved cherry tomatoes.
3. Drizzle the olive oil over the mixture and sprinkle with a pinch of sea salt. Toss to combine.
4. Top with slivered almonds and serve.

You'll get used to it.

Chapter 13

The Link Between a **Steak, a Cow, and My Diet**

I must confess, I've never fully grasped the relationship between a thin, crispy schnitzel on a plate and a live rooster, or between a juicy steak on the grill and a cow grazing in a meadow. Perhaps that's why I've never been a vegetarian in my life, and I didn't harbor guilt or moral doubts. Over the years, many of my friends transitioned to vegetarian and vegan diets, and I began to lean that way due to the perceived health benefits. I'm convinced, despite objections from the Paleo proponents, that food in its natural and unprocessed form, often harvested straight from the earth, is healthier. I've been intrigued for years, but I must admit I haven't permanently adopted this lifestyle change. After all, I live in the United States, the land of steaks and barbecues.

That all shifted one pivotal evening when I dined at a friend's house, who served an exclusively vegan meal. That's when I finally gave a sincere listen (having previously resisted, as I wasn't prepared to be swayed) to their explanations. Once I opened my ears to this novel way of life, I couldn't help but continue delving into it, watching brief and disconcerting videos about the meat industry and our food system. For some reason, a tiny fissure emerged in my defensive wall, a fissure that only broadened as the evening advanced. I returned home, binge-watched all the pro-vegan documentaries I could find until midnight, and made a resolution: we're starting tomorrow!

I must emphasize, though, that what ultimately swayed me towards veganism weren't moral considerations or health concerns. It was the before-and-after photos and the weight that seemed to effortlessly melt away from those who committed to a vegan lifestyle that sealed the deal. I hadn't tried it yet, and it appeared not only visually appealing but also ethically sound. So, what was I waiting for?

The next morning, a revolution occurred in our house: anything containing animal products was promptly handed over to our housekeeper. I then made few trips to the natural food stores, eagerly combing the shelves for enticing recipes and diligently noting down the essential ingredients for my new culinary journey. At that juncture in my life, my three children had already left the home and my husband, bless his heart, agrees to my every caprice (not that he had much of a choice). And that's how we ended up as die-hard vegans.

If there's one trait that characterizes me, for better or for worse, it's my "just do it" mindset. I was living by that mantra long before Nike adopted it as their slogan. Sometimes it serves me well, and other times a bit more contemplation and caution would be wise. But hey, that's just who I am.

Me, a Slave to Veganism

So, practically overnight, I found myself tied to the kitchen. I only have myself to blame, as I transformed into a round-the-clock culinary virtuoso. I dedicated hours to preparing vegetable dishes, lentils, quinoa, piping hot and chilled soups, smoothies, and vibrant juices—meals that were satiating without the load of empty carbs. The creativity required for such culinary adventures! My days were swallowed up by exploring markets, drying, chopping, steaming, grinding cashews for "cheese," mashing tofu, and juicing celery, kale, and parsley with an extra virgin (and extra costly) cold press juicer. Honestly, the food was so delicious and felt so energizing that I couldn't curb my appetite! I discovered a new, exciting world, and my body expressed its gratitude. I developed a relentless craving for green juices, açaí bowls sprinkled with nuts and oats, coconut butter chocolates, and ice cream made from bananas and dates. How could I possibly lose weight like this? Another book suggested eliminating all oils from my diet, so I recklessly complied—what could possibly go wrong? Then I bid goodbye to gluten (so long, bread, pizza crust, and pasta), and that suited me just fine! I replaced oil with cashew cream, bread with seed and avocado crackers, and suddenly my old calories were replaced by new ones. My weight stubbornly stayed the same.

Then, the coronavirus pandemic struck. Our children returned home for a few months, and I consider that period to be one of the most precious times of my life. We grew closer, detached from the distractions of the outside world. Conversations flowed around the grand wooden table during meals; in the evenings, we passed around a bottle of wine. There was no need for makeup or heels, and we were free from obligations and annoyances. We returned to the basics, to simplicity, to the warmth of family.

During this period, I had to cook for five adults, four of whom were blissfully well-adjusted and free of food-related neuroses. I cooked meals using ingredients I had ordered online, and more than once, I had to substitute apples with chicken breasts and quinoa with ice cream simply because that's what was available. My careful trips to health food stores, where I meticulously analyzed every product and label, became impossible. And so, almost magically, my strict veganism disappeared overnight, and we all relished the homemade dishes from the past.

There is no greater joy for me than preparing meatballs and mashed potatoes for my adult children, witnessing the nostalgia in their eyes as they remember their mother's and grandmother's cooking. I am a nurturing soul, and seeing empty plates warms my heart. As the pandemic eased, our children returned to their lives, and we resumed ours. Have I mentioned that living in extremes just isn't my style? So, even though I bid farewell to veganism, from time to time, I'm tempted to revisit it. And when I really feel the urge, I just say, "vegan schmegan" and treat myself to a juicy, grilled steak or some succulent ribs.

I've heard this approach referred to as "Flexitarian," derived from the word "flex"—meaning flexible. Well, at least for once in my life, I can say I'm flexible. It's no surprise that veganism didn't lead to weight loss, but it certainly enhanced my overall health and well-being, becoming an (occasional) lifestyle for me.

So, What's the Longevity Secret, Anyway?

Switching to veganism is just one piece of the puzzle. It's important to pay attention not only to what we eat, but also how and why. I won't get into the emotional aspect of eating here—I'll leave that to the experts. But when I learned about the "Blue Zones," I gained valuable insight into not only the "what," but also the "how."

What's the Blue Zones study? American journalist Dan Buettner, from National Geographic, set out to explore regions with the highest concentration of healthy, independent centenarians. These areas, pinpointed in the 1990s and identified by demographers Gianni Pes and Michel Poulain with blue circles, include Ikaria in Greece, Sardinia in Italy, Okinawa in Japan, Nicoya in Costa Rica, and Loma Linda in California.

Buettner aimed to meet these remarkable individuals, understand their lifestyles, and identify their common traits—without the need to learn Japanese or how to herd sheep in Greece. He wrote a global bestseller, *The Blue Zones: Lessons from the People Who've Lived the Longest, (11),* outlining nine principles we can incorporate into our lives for a longer, more joyful span of years.

Here are the nine principles, adapted for our contemporary lives, right here and now:

1. **Movement:** In none of the Blue Zones do people have gym memberships, practice Pilates on spring-loaded beds, or lift weights in a CrossFit box. They move naturally, walking up and down hills, spending a lot of time gardening and managing their homes and surroundings, and simply being active. Buettner suggests that we challenge ourselves: take the stairs instead of the elevator, park the car farther away and walk (in Tel Aviv, that's not really a problem; there's no parking anyway), or tend a garden in a yard or urban community. Just keep moving.
2. **Purpose:** All the residents of the Blue Zones have a sense of purpose in some form or another. Whether in Loma Linda, the heart of the Seventh-Day Adventists, or in Okinawa, where they coined the term Ikigai, meaning the intersection between what we love, what we excel at, what the world needs, and what we can make a living from. When all these elements align, we have found our Ikigai, and we actually never work a day in our lives.
3. **Downshifting:** Everyone experiences stress, but the residents of the Blue Zones know how to relax—whether through napping, meditating,

getting a good night's sleep, or taking a day off. How about a Saturday siesta or an annual vacation?

4. **Eat until 80 percent full:** Okinawans say "Hara hachi bu" before eating, reminding themselves to stop eating when they are 80 percent full. Maybe we could adopt a similar mantra or use chopsticks as a gentle reminder?
5. **Plant-based diets:** Blue Zones' inhabitants primarily consume plants, with occasional fish or meat. Buettner suggests that adding a daily half-cup of legumes to our diets could potentially increase our lifespan by seven years. So, let's embrace the flavors of nature and pretend that Diet Coke never existed.
6. **Wine at Five:** Well, I won't dispute whether wine is healthy or not. Those who don't drink shouldn't start, and this isn't a recommendation to start. But in all the Blue Zones (except Loma Linda), the residents enjoy a glass of local wine typically shared with friends. I wonder why I adopted this principle first. And no, there is no rollover policy for all the glasses of wine that you don't drink. It doesn't work that way.
7. **Finding the right tribe:** Various studies have shown that the habits of our close friends have a significant impact on us. So, it's important to choose

companions who support your desired lifestyle and spend quality time together. Maybe consider swapping out the sausage-eating club for a rowing team?

8. **Prioritizing family:** The residents of the Blue Zones dedicate a considerable amount of time to all generations of their families. Grandparents live with their children and grandchildren, they dine together, and they prioritize the family unit. Perhaps we should spend more time with our own families and embrace hobbies that can be enjoyed across different generations.
9. **Belonging:** Feeling a sense of belonging is crucial for our overall well-being. In Okinawa, people form lifelong groups called "moais" consisting of five members. These groups navigate through both the good and bad times, fostering loyalty and enduring bonds. We all need to feel that sense of belonging, even when we find ourselves in unfamiliar surroundings.

By incorporating some of these principles into our lives, we can potentially extend our lifespan and increase our overall happiness. But let's not rush into making radical changes. It's best to start small, perhaps by including three vegetarian meals a week or having a family meal without screens. Walking to the grocery store or going to bed an hour earlier without your phone can also make a positive difference. And don't forget to take a relaxing siesta on the weekends —it might be just what you need.

For Reflection and Self-Work

You can introduce some elements of the Blue Zones into your life today. These elements include diet, movement, sleep, finding meaning, finding your tribe, prioritizing family, and downshifting.

1. What Blue Zones principles can you incorporate into your life today?

2. How can you include movement and exercise in your daily routine?

For Reflection and Self-Work

3. What changes can you make to your diet to include more plant-based foods?

4. How can you introduce downshifting and rest in your busy schedule?

5. What intergenerational activities can you plan to prioritize family time?

6. How can you find and connect with like-minded people who share your values?

---

7. How can you find meaning and purpose in your life?

Recipe

A Life-Prolonging **Minestrone Soup** from Sardinia

To help you get started, here are two Blue Zones recipes courtesy of Dan Buettner, the journalist and author who researched the Blue Zones:

Ingredients:

- 1/2 cup dry chickpeas
- 1/2 cup dry white beans
- 1/2 cup dry pinto beans or red beans
- 1 and ½ cups diced potatoes
- 1/2 cup pearl barley (not for quick cooking)
- 1 can of chopped tomatoes or 5 date tomatoes
- 4 cups of water or vegetable stock for a richer taste
- 1 medium onion, chopped
- 5 celery stalks, finely chopped
- 5 carrots, chopped
- 8 garlic cloves, chopped
- 2 bay leaves
- 1 teaspoon of oregano
- 2 tablespoons of olive oil
- 1 teaspoon spicy red or black pepper
- Salt to taste

Recipe

A Life-Prolonging **Minestrone Soup** from Sardinia

Instructions:

Soak the beans overnight. If you forgot, you can cook the dry beans in the microwave in a bowl of water while you chop the other ingredients. Brown all the vegetables in olive oil over low heat. Add the hummus, beans, tomatoes, and water, and cook until the beans soften (for a faster soup, you can use a pressure cooker). You can let it cook on extremely low heat all day, and add water so that it's thicker than a soup but thinner than a stew. Add avocado and serve.

Recipe

A Slightly Spicy Bean **Burger**

Ingredients:

- 4 cups of cooked and drained beans (red or black or both), or canned beans, drained and rinsed
- 3/4 cup fresh whole grain breadcrumbs
- Up to 1 tablespoon hot red pepper sauce (such as Tabasco)
- 2 teaspoons chopped garlic
- 1/2 tablespoon Worcestershire sauce
- 1/2 teaspoon ground cumin
- 1/2 teaspoon salt
- Non-stick spray
- 4 whole grain hamburger buns
- 1/2 cup salsa
- 4 small lettuce leaves
- 4 slices of green pepper (optional)
- 4 thin red onion rings (optional)

Recipe

A Slightly Spicy Bean **Burger**

Instructions:

Put the beans, breadcrumbs, hot red pepper sauce, garlic, Worcestershire sauce, cumin, and salt in a large bowl. Use a potato masher to obtain a smooth paste. Cover and refrigerate for 30 minutes to solidify. Spray the grate of an outdoor gas grill with non-stick spray and heat to high heat, or spray a large grill pan with spray and heat over medium-high heat for a few minutes until very hot.

Meanwhile, with clean and wet hands, form 4 uniform patties from the bean mixture. Grill the patties for about 6 minutes until hot and slightly crispy, turning once. Place the patties on the bottom halves of the buns, top with 2 tablespoons of salsa each, place a lettuce leaf on top, and cover with the top halves of the buns. Garnish with pepper slices and onion rings as desired.

Remember to adopt these recipes and elements of the Blue Zones in a way that works for you, starting small and making gradual changes over time.

Thank you, Dan Buettner!

Chapter 14

Working Out and Other Tribulations

How I wish to be athletic, sporty, and well-toned! However, the reality is that I'm not. This is not to say that I haven't tried, or that I'm not still giving it my best shot. It just seems that in this lifetime, athleticism escapes me.

In my childhood, while my friends played sports and danced, my own form of exercise consisted of just enough movement to avoid colliding with walls while deeply absorbed in a book.

I've made numerous attempts throughout my life. As I prepare for my first Pilates class, which I'm attending soon, I feel compelled to share some of my experiences over the years that could easily rival my dieting attempts. I've already shared my ballet tales —let's continue.

Dance: I've sampled a variety, from jazz dancing (where the teacher barely noticed me), to folk dancing (where both the teacher and the dancers disregarded me), to a ballroom dancing class with my husband at the age of 45 (where the instructor kindly refunded our money). Despite these experiences, I find joy in dancing to disco, Motown, and Latin music.

I enjoy dancing to my own rhythm without choreography or repeating the teacher's movements, just the pure thrill of connecting to the music.

Basketball: I used to be a short girl, always positioned in the front row of class photos. But then, at the age of 15, I sprouted six inches in less than a year. The growth came with its own price—bone pain and noisy knees—diagnosed by various doctors as growing pains. Suddenly, I seemed tall enough to play basketball, so I joined the team. Unfortunately, my hands and feet didn't keep up with the growth spurt and remained small, which didn't really help with dribbling. Ultimately, my basketball journey ended as quickly as it started.

Years later, as I raised children in the U.S. and observed the inclusivity in sports (even my daydreaming son made it as a soccer team goalkeeper), I couldn't help but compare it to the meritocratic and elitist culture in Israel, where sports seemed reserved for the gifted. But that's a story for another time.

School gym classes: These bring up a painful memory. "Tami will not be able to participate in class today because she is not feeling well" was the routine note from my mother. I dreaded gym classes. Those gym shorts with the elastic band (those over 50 will surely remember them) linger in my memory.

The gym teacher would cast a glance my way, a blend of pity and disdain. Sprinting would end in defeat, and long-distance runs seemed to stretch into eternity. The long jump and high jump were indistinguishable to me, and during floor exercises, I'd find myself stuck in rolls, persistently trying to complete the maneuver. Can you picture it? That's how I grew up, believing sports were not my thing, and while my skinny brother could energetically run and play from dawn till dusk, it was clear that I hadn't inherited that same athletic gene.

The only game in which I truly excelled and surpassed all the other kids in the neighborhood was "corners." It involved tossing a ball at the opposite sidewalk and trying to make it hit the edge and rebound. How I became proficient in this game remains a mystery, but in my excitement, I managed spectacular performances, particularly in "back corners." In those moments, I felt like a true star—the best in a neighborhood that only had four kids.

Swimming: It occurred to me that swimming could be my forte—doing 30 laps every morning in the local community pool seemed like an excellent plan, and I enthusiastically brought a few friends on board. That neighborhood pool became iconic and an integral part of my childhood memories.

On the chosen day, I woke up early, slipped into my swimsuit, and made my way to the pool. The smell of chlorine and concrete still stays with me. We gathered at six in the morning, getting ourselves mentally prepared to dive into the cool water—what a wonderful feeling! So refreshing. There's truly nothing quite like swimming early in the morning. By seven, I was back home, surprising my mother with my dedication. I enjoyed a hearty breakfast and went to school feeling refreshed and full of energy. However, by ten o'clock, just before the bell rang for recess, you would find me and my three swimming buddies sound asleep. The exhaustion from swimming and lack of interest in our history class took its toll. As expected, our ambitious swimming venture came to an end on day one. But the enjoyable feeling of being in the water and the importance of exercise stuck with me, and I still do the occasional water aerobics to this day.

Could **military basic training** have been the turning point? The time came for me to enlist, and I was decidedly out of shape. Our training took place at the end of January, in freezing weather, and we slept in tents in the desert. Does the movie *Private Benjamin* with Goldie Hawn ring a bell? That was practically me. Besides struggling to rise from under a dozen coarse military blankets, fully clothed in my coat and trembling from the cold, I also struggled to keep up with the hikes and strenuous exercises. But there was no alternative. The army doesn't take kindly to notes from mothers. Therefore, I tried, exerted myself, perspired, fell, and ultimately, I persevered. At the end of a harsh hike on the rocky terrain, I concluded my training with a sprained ankle, my first disciplinary hearing, and an assignment to the Intelligence Corps, as far removed from physical exertion as one could possibly be.

As a student, my **university days** were defined not only by extreme diets, as I wrote about in the rice diet chapter, but also by a series of failed attempts to commit to physical activity. The solution, it seemed, arrived in the form of an elective course in Feldenkrais gymnastics. I felt a genuine connection with the tranquil, soothing act of alternately moving my left and right foot. But the part I most enjoyed was the Feldenkrais-style massage technique that we studied and practiced on each other using tennis balls. And that pretty much summed up my sports experiences as a student at Tel Aviv University.

Years later, I heard a rumor about a dear friend opening an innovative **passive exercise bed gym.** Incredible! He was always the genius! Naturally, I became his first and most faithful customer. I would visit four times a week, recline on one of the beds, and it would move on my behalf, simulating muscle contractions and stretches through its mechanical movements. One bed focused on my abs, another on my thighs, and I'd move from bed to bed for an hour, allowing each to work its magic. Two months later, the place declared bankruptcy (not too surprising), and I had to concede that I noticed no change in my muscular structure. Undeterred, I continued my quest for the perfect fitness fit.

Over time, I experimented with mat Pilates, reformer Pilates, yoga, scorching Bikram yoga, belly dancing, spinning, aqua spinning, personal training, and more. Sound familiar? Remind you of my diet list? You can clearly see I'm giving it my best try, right?

☛ Let's Reframe It

When I make the decision to start a particular exercise routine, it often feels like I'm setting myself up for failure. But that was then. Today, I have discovered a secret technique: Reframing. Rooted in psychology, reframing aims to create a new narrative and change our perception of a situation. This technique is used to uncover more optimistic perspectives in any given situation. For example, instead of telling myself that

I'm a bundle of nerves before a major event that I'm organizing, I reframe the situation and reassure myself that I'm overflowing with excitement for the event. Instead of dwelling on feelings of loneliness and boredom, I tell myself that I'm tranquil and serene. Each scenario has an alternative framing that is easier for us to accept. But how does this relate to me and exercise?

I don't strive for 10,000 steps a day, but I do take walks on the beach to contemplate my new course, hike in the woods to admire the colors of the foliage, or briskly walk to the other side of town to buy a rare ingredient from a specialty store for dinner. It's a much more enjoyable and engaging routine. In the pool, I dance to Zumba music, making it feel like a party rather than just swimming 50 laps. I know it's not the same, but it works for me. So, I aim to find two activities that I enjoy, that bring me joy, and that I find effortless. I alternate between them to avoid monotony and boredom (sorry, serenity).

And each day, I follow the advice of Dan Buettner, the "Blue Zones" researcher, who encourages us to inconvenience ourselves. Consequently, I try to park in the farthest parking space, take the stairs instead of the elevator, do some gardening or lift grocery bags. I feel a sense of accomplishment, knowing that by doing so, I have miraculously added years to my life!

For Reflection and Self-Work

1. How do you feel about exercise? Have you incorporated any physical activity into your routine, such as walking, running, cycling, swimming, going to the gym, or dancing?

2. If not, how can you identify one or two physical activities that you enjoy? What can you do tomorrow morning to start incorporating them into your routine?

3. How can you change your perspective on physical activities that you don't enjoy so that they bring you happiness? Can you reframe them in a positive way?

Recipe

Are you craving another recipe? This one is just as satisfying—a recipe for a delicious and effective **Aerobic Exercise in the Pool!**

Ingredients:

- A floating belt
- Water weights

Instructions:

First, put on the floating belt and get into the deep water. Your feet shouldn't touch the bottom. Then, for 45 minutes, listen to rhythmic music and try a variety of exercises such as walking, running, cross-country skiing, kicks, lifting your legs like a Rockette dancer, lifting weights in all directions, and marching. It's challenging, and you'll even break a sweat in the pool. However, exercising in water is easy on your joints, reduces cellulite, and fills your heart with joy.

Chapter 15

How Low Did I Go?

Throughout my conversations with friends, both female and male, I've come to realize that almost all of us have this little thing that consumes our thoughts and fantasies each day. It can be, and often is, something small and inconsequential, but to us, it seems enormous. We believe our whole lives would be different if only this one thing could change. I've heard it all: my hair is too thick or too thin, my legs are too far apart or too close, my nose is too long or crooked, my ears stick out, my skin, my smile. As we age, the list becomes even more specific: the furrow in the forehead, the sagging neck, the age spots on our hands, the varicose veins, the eyelids, and so on! How is this distinct from the 20 lbs. that stand between me and happiness as discussed in chapter 1? Here, the focus is on one tiny detail in the grand scheme of things. This particular sagging lid drives me crazy, and not necessarily aging overall.

For me, the one thing that kept me awake at night was my less-than-flat tummy. As a little girl, my mother used to pinch it like a toddler's cheek. "It's cute," she tried to reassure me, and as I grew older, "It's feminine." But nothing convinced me. I wanted a flat stomach. Does it sound petty? Superficial? Trivial? Yes, but what can I do? That's me, for better or worse. I'm sharing many of my secrets here in this book. I'm baring my soul and pouring it all out, so why not be completely open? No more skeletons in the closet.

My dream of tucking a shirt into my jeans with a chic belt was permanently relegated to the back burner after my third pregnancy, which ended in an emergency C-section. To save the baby, they had to cut quickly, not considering the mother's aesthetic wishes. When the muscles are severed, even 500 crunches a day won't help (not that I'd do that), and the dream of a flat stomach seemed more elusive than ever.

☛ Just a Consultation

So, at the age of 40, with three children and a C-section scar, I decided to take action. I went to consult a plastic surgeon.

To consult! Truly! Not to actually go under the knife,

God forbid! Just to listen! I was scared to even utter the words "tummy tuck" or "liposuction." It felt like insanity. To put myself at risk for elective surgery that could lead to so many complications. The doctor likely understood my apprehension, so he opted not to use the intimidating terminology. Instead, he downplayed them. A "mini tummy tuck" sounds much less daunting than a major surgery. A bit of "sculpting" is far less terrifying than liposuction. So, I left with a (tentative, of course) date for a minor enhancement. Truly minor.

"You're out of your mind," my friends told me. "What do you want? You have a husband and three wonderful children, and you're worried about such nonsense. What if something terrible happens? What if you don't wake up? What if, what if, what if . . ." And on the other hand: "Come on! Everyone does it. It's a little painful, but worth it. Nowadays, people get plastic surgery at a young age. She had a facelift and eye lift, and the other one sculpted her whole body. It's not that big of a deal anymore." And my mother: "You need a psychiatrist, not a plastic surgeon. What do you want from yourself?"

So, I really struggled, taking all scenarios into consideration, finding it very hard to decide, talking to myself on a daily basis:

On Sunday: "You're only 40 years old, and you have

many more years to live with something you despise (even if it's irrational), so go for it."

On Monday: "Are you out of your mind? You're not some superficial fool. A smart woman like you? You have a wonderful family. How could you even consider risking it? Drop it."

On Tuesday: "But if you don't do it now, it'll never happen. You're really only 40 and this belly looks dreadful. What could possibly go wrong? People can get hit crossing the street."

On Wednesday: "But are you willing to take such a risk? What are you lacking? You're just being spoiled."

So, for a month, I went back and forth, weighing the pros and cons. I consulted and inquired, pleaded for understanding, grew frustrated with myself, and felt embarrassed for even discussing it and wanting it so desperately. But I did want it so desperately!

So I went through with it.

And I woke up alive and kicking with a flat tummy.

And I was really happy until . . .

Next!

I loved how I looked, buying cowboy-style belts with flashy buckles, tucking my T-shirt in and becoming more of a fashionista than ever before. But then I started thinking to myself, "That went incredibly smoothly, so perhaps I could trim a bit more here? And tuck a tad more there?" (Don't worry, that's where I stopped). But suddenly, I noticed imperfections I hadn't seen before.

This is a well-known phenomenon when it comes to body enhancements, plastic surgeries, and beauty procedures. Fix one thing, and another seems to bother, and so we embark on the race for more. It's really never enough.

What does that remind you of? The "Hedonic Adaptation" from Chapter 2. In the world of plastic surgeries and procedures, this concept takes a powerful grip. Once your tummy is flat, your hips start to bug you. When your forehead is smooth, your eyes seem old. A wrinkle-free neck emphasizes aged hands, and so on and so forth. Where does it end? We see so many people around us who should have stopped a surgery or two ago but kept going. On the other hand, if fixing something that bothers you is feasible, why not?

I'm not here to argue for or against surgeries. I don't claim to fully understand someone else's body or invalidate their desires. But I've learned that when it comes to decisions involving tangible risk, it's important to approach them with reflection and responsibility. I also would like to remind you of the reframing technique, which worked against me in this case. A "mini surgery" is still a surgery, regardless of what you call it. Words may downplay the importance of the action, but not the outcomes and risks. I'm finished with deceiving myself, and if I'm ever tempted to try another "mini procedure," someone please remind me to be truthful with myself. Call a spade a spade and make a thoroughly considered decision.

For Reflection and Self-Work

1. Is there something small that bothers you a lot? What is it?

2. What steps are you willing to take to eliminate it?

3. What are the potential risks associated with taking action?

4. Are you prepared to accept those risks?

5. Are you using minimizing language to avoid confronting the truth about the situation?

Recipe

Overnight Oats
(I hear they help flatten your tummy)

Ingredients:

- 1/2 cup of old-fashioned oats (not quick-cooking)
- 2 tablespoons of chia seeds
- 1/2 cup of almond milk or regular milk
- A dash of vanilla extract
- 1 teaspoon of organic maple syrup or 1/2 frozen banana (for sweetness)

Instructions:

1. Combine all the ingredients in a jar with a lid and mix well.
2. Cover the jar and place it in the fridge overnight.
3. In the morning, mix the oats again and top with blueberries, sliced strawberries, shredded coconut, and crushed walnuts.

Enjoy your delicious and nutritious breakfast—much more pleasant than surgery!

Chapter 16

A Never Ending Story

This book's idea sparked over 15 years ago, in a rather unexpected way. During a corporate lunch I attended in my business development role, I happened to meet a colleague who, like me, opted for the chicken breast instead of pasta. She confessed that she had recently started a paleo diet and was avoiding carbs.

"Heard of it?" she asked.

"Yes, I know them all," I replied, and added, "in fact, I'm writing a book about them."

I meant it as a figure of speech, of course, trying to imply that my extensive knowledge of diets could fill a book. But her eyes lit up, and she eagerly asked, "Really? What's the title of the book?"

Playing along with the playful banter, I responded, "How to Be on a Diet for 30 Years and Never Be Thin." To me, it sounded like a funny parody of those American "How to . . ." books. But she took me seriously and exclaimed, "Wow, that sounds fantastic.

When's it coming out?" That's when I decided that despite having no prior writing experience and my initial intention being a joke, I would actually write this book.

Every time we saw each other afterwards, she would ask, "How's the book coming along?"

"Oh, just writing away," I'd respond, even though that couldn't have been further from the truth. "You really need to finish it soon. I can't wait to read it." That's when I realized that there might be genuine interest in such a book. After all, I already had one enthusiastic reader!

The truth is I kept putting off the writing process because I was always starting something new—a new diet, method, injection, or support group—and I genuinely believed that it would work, that things would turn around. But they never did . . . and the title of the book continued getting updated to "How to Be on a Diet for 40 Years . . ." with each passing year, and I was worried it would become outdated. But that didn't happen. It's still relevant, and here's the latest update from the front lines: I'm still stuck in neutral. There are no new before-and-after photos (at least not in the usual order), and here we are, two months into the three-month commitment to finally fit into that little black dress for my 60th birthday. Between you and me, I'm still trying because I made a promise, but the scale hasn't budged. As it says on the cute apron I once received as a gift: "I'm on a 30-day diet. I've already lost two weeks." So maybe I should consider that injection everyone's been talking about?

Do you remember the film *The NeverEnding Story*? It's a beautiful tale about a story within a story, trapped in a loop that repeats itself endlessly. Based on my past experiences, I can't help but feel like the main character in that film.

The Rock in Buddha's Garden

Don't worry, I've purchased a loose-fitting outfit for my birthday, and it's slowly becoming clear to me that if it hasn't happened by now— it's a sign! The truth is, I'm growing a bit weary of stepping on the scale, cringing at the thought of those extra 10 lbs. lost after Herculean efforts, only to see them return after an evening out or my first venture to a restaurant. Suddenly, things take on a different perspective, especially as the number of yesterdays on the calendar starts to outweigh the tomorrows.

I strongly believe in the concept of "The Rock in Buddha's Garden." The idea is that perfection, like Buddha's Zen garden, is impossible to achieve. There has to be one thing that's imperfect, one rock jutting out in the beautiful garden. For me, fortunately, it's just 20 extra lbs. Or maybe they serve some divine purpose in my understanding? As my mother used to say, "Until the fat gets thin, the thin dies." Either way, if something has to be flawed, I'd rather it be my weight and not, heaven forbid, something else like health, family, relationships, or livelihood.

And maybe I am who I am because of these 20 lbs., because of this imperfection? As Brené Brown, an American researcher, lecturer, and author, writes in her excellent book, *The Gifts of Imperfection (15)*: "When we stop trying to be someone else or striving for perfection, we become people who work from the heart. In the journey from "I am not enough . . ." to "This is me, this is what I have, this is good enough," we develop the three most important heart-based qualities: courage, compassion, and human connection."

So, I embrace them.

Courage means publishing this book, admitting I'm not perfect, and starting a conversation from a new and different place that resonates with so many of us in different ways. Compassion means showing kindness toward myself and others who face challenges that make them feel incomplete and imperfect. Human connection means understanding that we're all connected, part of the same world, rather than isolated islands. I'm grateful to be able to help others through introspection, advice, and tips drawn from my own experiences, with plenty of humor, love, and empathy.

Who knows what path my life would have taken if I had been the homecoming queen? Would I feel perfect? Maybe I wouldn't have developed my personality to the same extent. Maybe I wouldn't have touched as many hearts as I have.

God has plans.

So, I'm going to enjoy my life and freedom journey. I'll keep laughing at myself, knowing it doesn't make sense to constantly obsess over anything, let alone 20 pounds! I'll go on living happily and appreciate all the good things life has given me, while still looking for the next solution, trying almost anything that comes my way—because I still want to be thin! And my 65th birthday is already smiling at me on the horizon. I don't have any groundbreaking news or solutions. I haven't reinvented myself as a triathlete or adopted a lifestyle that made me lose weight. I've just embraced a healthy 80 percent way of life, but I don't always carry a percentage calculator. Some days, I'm 110 percent good; other days, not so much. That's me—and I love myself just the way I am. (Like I have any choice?) Did I mention I'm comfortable in the grey area? In the middle? So I've shifted a bit, but I'm still far from black and white. The most valuable lesson I've learned through the years and from writing this book is that I am the only one who controls my life, who dictates my experience. I decide if I should attend to the voices or ignore them, love myself or not, develop and flourish or become bitter and stuck.

☛ **It's my life! My freedom.**

And what did you, dear reader, take away from the book? Did you see a bit of yourself in it? Did you suddenly open an old photo album and realize you had actually been stunning all along? Did you discover that you were charming and captivating all these years? Maybe you chuckled a bit with me about yourself? Or just at me? Perhaps you skipped straight to the insights because you realized there were genuinely useful life tools you could start applying? Or went directly to the recipes because you just started a ketogenic diet? And maybe, casually, you placed the book next to your daughter's bed to spare her some unnecessary agony? Whatever it is—I did my part.

I have a feeling we're not parting ways for good, but just for a while, until there's enough material for a sequel or a stand-up act. I already miss you!

☛ Who's the Happy One Now?

We all have much to be grateful for. Sonia Lyubomirsky, a renowned happiness researcher, found a direct link between gratitude and an individual's happiness and mental resilience. Joe Cocker's lyrics paint a vivid picture: standing knee-deep in a river, dying of thirst. We're often surrounded by abundance, yet fail to see it. What's the opposite of gratitude? I believe it's "taking things for granted." We become accustomed to our blessings to the point where we stop appreciating our surroundings and what we have.

Research consistently shows we learn to appreciate what we have only when it's lost or under threat. People tell me, "I actually know how to be grateful." Is that true? Deep down to the cells of your body? Do you whisper before sleep, "Wow, I'm one lucky person?" Not always, not truly. Gratitude doesn't always come naturally, like running doesn't come naturally to me. But it can and should be practiced. If you take only one thing from this book, let it be this—a gratitude journal. With a mere two to three minutes a day, it can greatly enhance your happiness. Give it a try!

So where did this idea come from? Over 20 years ago, American author Sarah Ban Breathnach wrote *Simple Abundance* (13) and spoke about the importance of practicing gratitude daily. She made various attempts to reach Oprah Winfrey (who wouldn't?), even strategically placing her books in Winfrey's staff members' rooms, hoping one would pass it on to Oprah. It worked. Breathnach eventually appeared on Oprah's highly regarded show, introduced the world to the concept of simple abundance, and popularized the gratitude journal. Oprah loved it, and the rest is history. This practice is now recognized as a powerful tool in the field of positive psychology.

How does it work? Each night before going to sleep, write down or reflect on five things you're grateful for that day. These can be significant things like family, home, the life you can afford, your parents, or smaller, fleeting things: a successful new recipe, a feel-good movie, a missed-you message from a loved one, or resisting the temptation of that Cherry Garcia ice cream. Some nights, you may simply express thanks for the day passing and a new day ahead. If five things feel like too much, start with three. The key is to practice regularly (whether daily or weekly) and do it with intention, almost like a prayer. Relive the feelings, tastes, and love associated with those moments of gratitude.

Why does this practice work so well? How does such a quick exercise have a profound impact on our happiness not just during the moment, but throughout the entire day? First, knowing that we need positive things to recall at night makes us more attuned to finding the positives throughout the day. Suddenly, our glasses appear rosier. Instead of falling asleep with thoughts about tomorrow's chores or today's problems, we fall asleep with a heart full of positivity and a smile.

The sages were indeed correct when they said, "How rich is one who's content with their lot?" In every situation, there is always something to be grateful for —it should never be taken for granted.

So why not embrace gratitude? Sure, I may still be struggling with those extra 20 pounds, but if my journey has taught me anything, it's that life is about finding joy in small moments and appreciating what we have. As I fill my gratitude journal, I have come to realize that happiness is not about perfection or having it all; it is about acknowledging imperfection and celebrating the everyday.

So, dear reader, as you turn the last page of my weight-loss memoir, I hope that you take away a piece of wisdom, share a hearty laugh, and develop a renewed appreciation for the simple abundance that surrounds you. Embrace gratitude, and who knows, you might discover that happiness is closer than you ever imagined.

For Reflection and Self-Work

1. What general things are you grateful for in your life?

2. What have you been taking for granted?

3. One thing that happened today that you will put into your gratitude journal tonight?

And as for me, I am grateful for you.
Thank you for sharing laughter, compassion, and love with me. I appreciate you opening up to this experience and looking at yourselves **with more compassion.**

Thank you for listening and supporting me.
Tonight, you will be in my gratitude journal.
Nice to have met you.
I'm Tami Muller,
and I am both whole and imperfect.

Recipe

So what do I leave you with?
Some super simple and healthy recipes that are both delicious and easy to prepare.

Cold Soup (Gazpacho) with a Twist

Ingredients:

- 2 green cucumbers with the skin
- 2 tomatoes
- 1 red bell pepper
- 1 cup of watermelon
- 1/2 red onion
- 1 clove of garlic
- 1 slice of wholewheat bread
- 1 tablespoon of red or white wine vinegar
- 1/4 cup of cold-pressed olive oil

Instructions:

1. Mix all the ingredients in a strong blender.
2. Chill the soup in the fridge.
3. Serve with a spoonful of Greek yogurt.

Recipe

Asian-Style Salmon in the Oven

Ingredients for the marinade:

- 1/4 cup soy or tamari sauce
- 2 tablespoons of honey or organic maple syrup
- 2 cloves of garlic
- 1 piece of fresh ginger root
- 1 tablespoon of balsamic vinegar

Ingredients for the fish:

- Salmon fillet
- 1 chopped green onion
- Sesame seeds

Instructions:

1. Combine the ingredients for the marinade in a blender.
2. Pour the marinade over the salmon fillet and refrigerate for at least an hour.
3. Bake at 350F for 15–20 minutes.
4. Sprinkle with sesame seeds and chopped green onions.

Recipe

Unstoppable Seed Crackers with Vegan Miso Butter

Ingredients for the crackers:

- 1 cup of ground flax seeds
- 1 cup of raw sunflower seeds
- 1/2 cup of chia seeds
- 1/2 cup of hemp seed
- 1/4 cup of raw sesame seeds
- 1/2 cup of almond flour
- 2 tablespoons of coriander seeds
- 2 egg whites
- 2 cups of water
- 1 teaspoon of sea salt

Instructions:

1. Preheat the oven to 350F degrees.
2. Mix all the ingredients in a bowl.
3. Flatten the mixture with wet hands until a smooth and thin surface is formed.
4. Bake for 45 minutes.
5. Turn off oven and leave inside to dry.
6. Break into pieces and store in a box in the freezer.

Recipe

Unstoppable Seed Crackers with Vegan Miso Butter

Ingredients for the vegan miso butter:

- 2 heaping tablespoons of white miso
- Juice of 1 lemon
- 1 cup of unroasted cashews soaked in water for several hours
- 1/3 cup of water
- 1 tablespoon raw tahini

Instructions:

1. Mix all the ingredients in a food processor or blender.
2. Store in the refrigerator.

Recipe

Satisfying Healthy Salad to Keep in the Fridge— Even for a Couple of Days

Ingredients:

- 2 carrots
- 4 cucumbers or 1 long English cucumber
- A bunch of radishes
- 1 uncooked beetroot
- 3 stalks of celery
- A bunch of cilantro

Instructions:

1. Wash the vegetables and grate them in a food processor.
2. Store in the fridge.
3. Add olive oil, lemon, or homemade mayonnaise before serving.

Recipe

Homemade Mayonnaise

Ingredients:

- 1 egg
- 1 teaspoon of Dijon mustard
- 1 teaspoon of lemon juice or apple cider vinegar
- A pinch of salt
- 2 cups of extra light olive oil

Instructions:

1. Mix all the ingredients except for the oil in a food processor.
2. Slowly add the oil while mixing.
3. Store in the fridge.

Recipe

Nectarine Crumble

Ingredients:

- 2 lbs. of nectarines, peaches, or plums—or a mix of them
- Juice of 1 lemon
- 1/4 cup of cornstarch
- Optional: brown sugar to taste

Ingredients for the crumble:

- 1/2 cup flour
- 1/2 cup of unsalted butter or coconut oil
- 1/4 cup of organic maple syrup
- 1/2 cup of raw walnuts or almonds, chopped

Recipe

Nectarine Crumble

Instructions:

1. Preheat oven to 375F.
2. Mix the nectarines with lemon juice and cornstarch.
3. Spread the mixture in a baking dish.
4. Mix all the ingredients for the crumble and spread it over the fruit.
5. Bake for about 40 minutes.
6. Serve with vanilla ice cream or "nice cream" made from blended frozen bananas.

Well, I'm ready to host and be hosted.
And what's the event I'm about to break
a diet for now?
When this book I've been writing in my head
for ten years finally gets published!

Bibliography

1. Neff, K. (2011). *Self-Compassion: The Proven Power of Being Kind to Yourself.* William Morrow Paperbacks.
2. Atkins, R. C. (1981). *Dr. Atkins' Diet Revolution.* Bantam.
3. Lyubimirsky, S. (2008). The How of Happiness: A Scientific Approach to Getting the Life You Want. Penguin Books.
4. Baumeister, R. (1998). Radish and Chocolate. *Journal of Personality and Social Psychology.*
5. Cooperrider, D. L., & Whitney, D. (2005). *Appreciative Inquiry: A Positive Revolution in Change.* Berrett - Koehler Publishers.
6. Kempton, B. (2018). Wabi *Sabi: Japanese Wisdom for a Perfectly Imperfect Life.* Little, Brown Book Group.
7. Donne, J. (1959). *Devotions upon Emergent Occasions Together with Death's Duet.* The University of Michigan Press.
8. Mineo, L. (2017, April 11). *Good genes are nice but joy is better.* The Harvard Gazette.
9. Ben-Shahar, T. (2007). *Happier: Learn the Secrets of Daily Joy and Lasting Fulfillment.* The McGraw - Hill Companies.

10. Milgram, S. (1963). *Behavioral study of obedience.* The Journal of Abnormal and Social Psychology, 67(4), 371-378.
11. Buettner, D. (2011). *The Blue Zones: Secrets for Living Longer, Lessons From the Healthiest Places on Earth. National Geographic.*
12. Brown, B. (2010). *Gifts of Imperfection.* Hazelden Information & Educational Services.
13. Ban Breathnach, S. (1995). *Simple Abundance: A Daybook of Comfort.* Warner Books.

Acknowledgments

The journey of bringing this book to life was made possible by the unwavering help, love, and support I received along the way.
Special thanks to:

- Dr. Moshe Ben-Eliezer: for believing in me when I didn't believe in myself.
- Dr. Tal Ben-Shahar: my mentor and teacher, who showed me the true meaning of courage.
- Yuval Abramovich: for providing the final push and making it all happen.
- Gabe: for translating and editing my story with a son's unique love and remarkable talent.
- Robert Mitchell: for his graceful and patient guidance that I will forever be grateful for.
- Einav Shachar: for all the talent and love she put into making it beautiful.
- Iris, my sister: for sharing more than 60 years of this incredible journey.
- Bernie Gonzales: for sparking the idea with a simple question about dieting.
- Jordan McCrary: for enthusiastically introducing this book to the world.

- To my dear friends who supported, listened, and helped me along this extended journey: Irit Perlman, Lea Shani, Sarah Abraham, Zion Zohar, Karin Regev, Judy Oppenheim, Smadar Katzman, Orly Shiv and many, many more.

- Dani, Gabe, Yoni and Avia: my amazing family, who read this book numerous times in every language and still find joy in it, making me feel truly blessed.

ISBN 9798218333348

9 798218 333348

90000 >

How to Be on a Diet for 45 Years and Never Be Thin

A Practical Guide to Freedom and Happiness

Tami Muller

Printed in Great Britain
by Amazon

53666668R00126